D1086267

DEAD AGAIN

V

DEAD AGAIN

The Russian Intelligentsia After Communism

MASHA GESSEN

VERSO

London · New York

First published by Verso 1997
© Masha Gessen 1997
All rights reserved

Verso
UK: 6 Meard Street, London W1V 3HR
USA: 180 Varick Street, New York NY 10014–4606

Verso is the imprint of New Left Books

ISBN 1–85984–841–9
ISBN 1–85984–147–3 (pbk)

British Library Cataloguing in Publication Data
A catalogue record for this book is available from the British Library

Library of Congress Cataloging-in-Publication Data
Gessen, Masha.
  Dead again: the Russian intelligentsia after Communism/Masha Gessen
     p.   cm.
  Includes bibliographical references and index.
  ISBN 1–85984–841–9 (hardcover). — ISBN 1–85984–147–3 (pbk.)
  1. Russia (Federation) — Intellectual life — 1991– I. Title.
  DK510.56. G47 1997
947.086—dc21   97–3922
                                                        CIP

Typeset by CentraCet Ltd, Cambridge
Printed by Biddles Ltd, Guildford and King's Lynn

To the success of our hopeless mission

CONTENTS

ACKNOWLEDGMENTS

There are a number of people I must thank. Malcolm Imrie at Verso first floated the idea and then was more attentive and patient than I dared hope. My agent, Ellen Geiger at Curtis Brown in New York, was an ideal American intermediary between a Russian author and a British publisher.

My biggest debt, of course, is to the many people interviewed for this book, who, for reasons that sometimes remained a mystery to me, took time out of their schedules to talk and talk and talk with me. And I am very grateful to Yelena Chernykh and Laima Geidar, who deciphered some of the tapes of those conversations.

Richard Schimpf read the manuscript and aided me greatly in moving along, not only with his invariably useful editorial comments but with his unfailing friendship – a friendship that has played such an important part in my life for the last six years. Konstantin Gessen plowed through the manuscript in record speed, making always necessary if not always pleasant comments, all the while delighting his big sister with his skill and intelligence. Dave Tuller trained a keenly nit-picky editorial eye on the manuscript, benefiting it beyond measure.

There are several people who may not realize how much their confidence in me and my ability has meant. They are Laurie Essig, Dave Tuller, Arben Kastrati, everyone at the dacha, and especially my father, Alexander Gessen, whose pride in my work is sufficient reward in itself.

Finally, there is one person without whom I might not have survived, much less finished this book. My partner, Kate Griffin, cared for me when I had a hole in the head and cared about me when she may have wished to put one there herself. A thankless job, but I give my thanks.

At temple's entrance, in the snow
She stands alone. She shivers, cold.
In tattered clothing, fallen low,
The beggar is pathetic, old.

The tide of history has mauled her.
Oh! how quickly things can change.
Intelligentsia, they called her.
So, brother, can you spare some change?

She was not worker, was not peasant.
She manufactured nothing. Yet,
She bore the burden 'til the present:
For all she answered with her head.

They whipped and maimed her, killed her. And
They kicked her to lands frightful, strange.
A "subclass" she was called in this land.
So, brother, can you spare some change?

She stood in galleries, immobile;
For libraries she crafted books.
She taught our children to be noble,
And now she chooses: beg or hook.

She cries a lot, and nothing's funny
As a result of market change
She's lost her status and her money,
So, brother, won't you spare some change?

✕

She made us all so rich in spirit,
And now is poorer than us all.
Could it be that we cannot hear it –
Or we no longer need her call?

We'll plunge to barbarous new lows
When we have driven her to where
They still want minds and talent. So
I ask whatever you can spare.

She's fragile, starving and pathetic.
She has no means to live as such,
But she goes to the theater, maintains her ethic.
She reads, she smokes, and she drinks too much.

In any wake of any trouble
Intelligentsia will be:
You'll see her shape amid the rubble –
What's left from struggle to be free.

At temple's entrance, in the snow
She stands alone. She shivers, cold.
In tattered clothing, fallen low,
Intelligentsia is old.

A parody of a poem by Pierre Jean de Béranger, written by Vladimir Pankov and Mark Rozovsky and performed by the Moscow theatre U Nikitskikh vorot (By the Nikitsky Gate) in a show starting in the early 1990s. Each time the song is performed, by a small actress clad in pathetic rags, part of the audience storms the stage to deposit money in the actress's tattered black hat. Many nights bring in more in such donations than the troupe would otherwise make in a week.

Translated by Konstantin and Masha Gessen

PART ONE

A BRIEF HISTORY OF THE INTELLIGENTSIA

Boris, I do not like the intelligentsia and I do not consider myself a member of it.

        — Marina Tsvetaeva, letter to Boris Pasternak

A tiny old woman sat on the daybed, rocking slowly from side to side, her stare fixed somewhere to my left. To my right, a boom-box blared radio news; beyond it, a television set, muted in anticipation of the news, flickered through the dusty air.

"The apartment is a mess," she had said when I came in. "I think, *There is a war on. Why should I clean?*"

I had known Larisa Bogoraz for about a year and a half. We'd met on a human rights fact-finding mission to Russian prisons, and she had won the hearts and minds of the entire ten-person delegation — in which everyone else was at most half her age — with her extraordinary drive to discuss. Chain-smoking foul-smelling hollow-filter cigarettes, racked by a cough that threatened to break her body in half, she kept us up through long nights of discussion, intent on borrowing knowledge with the sort of urgency that suggested that if the world ended tomorrow, she could not die without learning our opinions on, say, the state of Russian news journalism. Of course, observing her, we all feared that was precisely what was about to happen. She was barely sixty but looked eighty. She had spent years in Siberian exile, had lost two husbands to the Gulag, and had faced various forms of persecution for over two decades. In fact, our mission coincided with the twenty-fifth anniversary of the demonstration in Red Square protesting the Soviet invasion of Czechoslovakia — one of the most dramatic milestones of the dissident movement; she had been one of the seven demonstrators. Twenty-five years later, she looked

3

poised to collapse but seemed to have more energy than any of the rest of us: during our late-night discussions, the younger participants would doze off one after another while Bogoraz kept going. The next day, we would be struggling to rub our eyes free of sleep while hers always looked alert and full of interest.

Now I saw her eyes dull, devoid of not only interest but hope. She no longer seemed a giant force contained in a frail body; she looked like she was hardly there. "It's all our fault," she intoned, rocking. "We propped up this regime – we, human rights activists. It's all our fault."

Like other members of the dissident movement – or at least the best-known part of it, the liberal intelligentsia – who had spent their lives in opposition to the regime and the authorities, Bogoraz had in the last several years been allowed to get progressively closer to the institutions of power. After decades of speaking their minds around the kitchen table, this group of people were given a national pulpit and led to believe that they were playing a key role in toppling the regime that had imprisoned them and repressed their ideas. They had believed the Soviet system to be the root and residence of evil in their country. In the cause of its destruction, these people, inexperienced in political machinery, were willing to make unlikely alliances and close their eyes to some of the tactics used. Most of them lent their crucial support to President Boris Yeltsin in October 1993, when his troops shelled the Russian Supreme Soviet building, with rebellious members of the pro-Communist parliament inside. "It's all our fault," Bogoraz was saying now. "We were so sick of the Soviet regime that we thought it should be destroyed by any means. So we supported Yeltsin, making him think he could do anything."

The particular sort of despair that I saw in Bogoraz's eyes that day I would see again and again. A few days later I went to cover the war in Chechnya, where I traveled with the Russian human rights commissioner, Sergei Kovaliov, himself a former dissident who had spent nearly a decade in prison camps, and his team of human rights researchers, at least half of whom were also long-time dissidents. For all of them, the war in Chechnya spelled the death of their dreams. It was an incredible feat for the regime: to kill hope in a group of people who had somehow kept it alive through imprisonment, forced exile and murder of their loved ones, through pervasive repression that had lasted decades, through a struggle that would have looked hopeless to anyone but them. Now, in January 1995, every evening they would gather at a hotel about an hour away from the devastated Chechen capital of Grozny and exchange their impressions of the day, with someone invariably proposing the traditional dissident toast "to the success of our hopeless mission" – now pronounced without a trace of irony or, for that matter, hope.

Like Bogoraz, they blamed themselves. In their minds, their duty lay in educating and ennobling the government. They had been trying all their lives, and now they were subjected to the cruelest punishment imaginable: they watched people dying as a result of what they believed was their own failure. They said things that sounded incongruous in these surroundings. At a press conference held in the unheated presidential palace in Nazran, the capital of the neighboring republic of Ingushetia, Mikhail Molostvov, a Parliament member who first became a political prisoner in the 1950s, related his impressions after spending a month in Grozny while the city was being shelled. "For us, who grew gray in a city under siege, for us, who saw the children crying, for us, reared on Russian literature, which taught us that world harmony is not worth shedding a single child's tear – " Quoting the most famous line from *The Brothers Karamazov*, he trailed off momentarily, while his audience of about fifty shivering, mud-splattered war correspondents struggled to follow the line of his narrative. "If the intelligentsia of Russia is going to treat Dostoyevsky's tenet regarding a child's tear as some kind of a transcendent ideal having no application in real life, the political degradation of this country will continue." Later, at the hotel, the gray-bearded Molostvov said simply, "We, the intelligentsia, are responsible for all of this completely."

"We the intelligentsia" is a phrase of unparalleled resilience and gravity. Isaiah Berlin called the concept of the intelligentsia "arguably Russia's greatest contribution to world civilization." Since the birth of the phenomenon in the 1830s, thousands of men and women have found in

it the meaning of their lives, their inspiration and the name of their calling, and have proceeded to struggle and suffer under the weight of the responsibility it entailed.

In August 1995 I went to Warsaw to attend a Slavic studies congress that was meant to open with a large plenary discussion on the intelligentsia and its role in contemporary Russian society. When I arrived, I discovered that the plenary had been downgraded to a small workshop. At the workshop it seemed to me I understood why this had happened: in the eyes of observers, the once-glorious concept had become comical. The scholars and writers on the panel, painfully aware of the need to define their subject, incessantly cracked self-conscious jokes.

"It is the Russians' favorite citation from the *OED*," opined the Englishman, referring to the dictionary entry identifying *intelligentsia*'s roots as Russian.

"I have never met a Russian who did not believe himself to belong to the intelligentsia," added the American to a roomful of giggles.

"How wonderful it is," responded the Russian, as though delivering the punch line of a tedious intercultural joke, "to spend your life talking about yourself, all the while insisting that you do not exist or are dying."

It is certainly easier laughingly to outline the contours of the phenomenon that is the intelligentsia than to define it seriously – not because it eludes definition but because its classical description is so somber, so high-minded, so earnest that in the 1990s it would certainly seem more appropriate to a war zone than to a contemporarily self-conscious scholarly conference. Though, of course, in the actual war zone, all talk of the intelligentsia seemed almost frivolously out of place.

The concept of the intelligentsia takes root with a small group of educated young men who lived by Hegel and the German Romantics and believed that it was their calling in life to bring about the enlightenment of their country. Very particular forces came together to produce this sense of responsibility, what Berlin calls the "collective sense of guilt," that the intelligentsia has carried with it for a century and a half.

First, Russia was – and, in ways now more difficult to define but no less perceptible for that, continues to be – a country rigidly divided into the very few who possess a certain sort of formal knowledge and the masses who do not. Second, from the time of Peter the Great it was impressed upon the country that enlightenment, which came from abroad, was the land's future and its salvation. The privileged few who had access to distant, expensive knowledge thought of themselves as conduits of light and felt a grave personal responsibility for their country's ultimate fate.

With the exception of the briefest periods when the intelligentsia may be considered to have shared in state power, two modes of relating to the regime fought for dominance among the intelligentsia. One opposed the regime and would topple it. The other condemned some actions of the regime and would enlighten it. Either way, the intelligentsia drew its identity in part from its relationship to and its distance from the regime.

Everything the intelligentsia did, it did in the name of the People. Indeed, all great internal Russian struggles raged over the fate of a mythical People as a whole. Members of the intelligentsia devoted great amounts of ink and time to refining the image of the People for which they toiled. But there was little they could do to disguise their utter ignorance and resulting fear of the great unwashed. Thus the second factor that defined the intelligentsia's place in society was its fearful distance from the People.

Possibly because the regimes, even as they succeeded one another, continued to be repressive and unenlightened, the intelligentsia, as a concept, lived through the turmoil of history. The intelligentsia suffered the crimes of the regime – and these were numerous – as its own failures. It protested, issuing words of pain, shame and hope against hope. The regime censored the words, thereby granting them an importance far beyond the impact a small group of the differently minded could be expected to have in a vastly indifferent land.

To be sure, the intelligentsia changed, experiencing crises of identity and faith and proclaiming its own demise with staggering regularity. After the first Russian revolution in 1905, two distinct camps emerged within the intelligentsia. One was an atheist group oriented toward the West in very much the same way as the first crop of the intelligentsia in the 1830s. The other warned loudly against the dangers such a mentality posed to Russia's moral fabric. In 1909 the latter group published a collection of essays called *Vekhi* (Milestones), issuing its caution.

Inasmuch as the October 1917 revolution was a triumph of the radical part of the atheist, Marxist wing of the intelligentsia, the split grew deeper. A large part of the intelligentsia was faced with yet another apparently lethal crisis. In a 1922 article entitled "On Militant Material-ism," Lenin essentially declared war on the "reactionary" intelligentsia, claiming that "professors and writers" were "obvious counterrevolution-aries . . . spies, the molesters of youth." Declared *personae non gratae* in a time of extreme hardship, scores of intellectual professionals, including about a quarter of the members of the Russian Academy of Sciences, died of hunger in the years immediately following the October Revolution. In 1922, the secret police, directed by Lenin and the Politburo, packed 160 scholars – among them most of the *Vekhi* authors – onto a steamship that delivered them to foreign exile. The ship went down in historical lore as the Philosopher Steamer. Hundreds of other prominent thinkers and writers exited by other transport. The remaining intelligentsia and the regime began a strange new dance.

Just as the Soviets were purging the disobedient intellectuals, a new trend was born among the intelligentsia. A collection of *émigré* articles published in Prague in 1921 and entitled *Smena vekh* (A Change of Milestones) advocated conciliation with the Bolsheviks. Apparently inspired in part by this and similar books, many members of the intelligentsia returned to Soviet Russia in the early 1920s.

In the course of the first decade following the revolution, the new regime nationalized all cultural production, ordering strict adherence to certain styles and even genres. The art schools that had proclaimed revolutionary ideas most passionately – the Constructivists, the Futurists – fell into violent disfavor. A utilitarian classicism was decreed the Soviet style: that is, grand form that served ideological content. The leader of the Constructivists, Kazimir Malevich, succumbed, attempting toward the end of his life to change his entire way of painting. The great Futurist poet, Vladimir Mayakovsky, committed suicide. So did many other artists of all schools; those who did not often suffered tragically, ending their days in labor camps, as did the poet Osip Mandelstam, or living in poverty watching the arrests and torment of loved ones, as did the poet Anna Akhmatova.

Next the Soviets nationalized scholarship. Textbooks in all fields proclaimed Joseph Stalin the chief expert in the area. He claimed the honor of being the world's greatest linguist and the top expert in biology. Certain schools of thought within disciplines were decreed correct. In biology, for example, it was the Lysenko doctrine, which held that lifestyle affected genetic makeup (it would logically follow that it was possible to create the Brave New Man of the Brave New World). No scholarly work in any field could be considered valid without references to Marxist-Leninist philosophical tracts and the Great Scholar himself.

The worker bees of this intellectual environment were later dubbed – by the intelligentsia itself – "the Soviet intelligentsia," *Soviet* being less a geographical or even ideological appellation than one denoting possession. They were not the regime, but they carried out the regime's orders and held Soviet science – a great source of international prestige – and scholarship on their shoulders. They often worked for a Big Idea – either the Big Soviet Idea or a private Big Idea that justified participating in the lies of the regime. That is, that part of the Soviet establishment that was its intelligentsia continued to suffer some mutation of the intelligentsia's moral torment.

Throughout Stalin's reign, concurrently with the purges that hit the intelligentsia, including that part of it that was loyal to the regime, the Soviets began creating structures for rewarding the intelligentsia both morally and materially. Those engaged in intellectual pursuits enjoyed a relative level of comfort unparalleled in the Western world. Officially recognized writers – those accepted into the Writers' Union – were granted special living quarters, luxurious resorts, better-quality medical care and even had their own excellent restaurants in the major cities. Hundreds of thousands of men and women were able to spend their lives engaged in vague scholarly pursuits. Thousands of research institutes paid out salaries to innumerable research staff who enjoyed flexible schedules and minimal accountability.

The moral remuneration was probably much more significant for the professional intellectuals. Research work, intellectual activity afforded a great deal of prestige. When I was a small child, my father, then thirty, bought a motorcycle and went to register it with the traffic inspection. "Comrade Gessen," the traffic policeman addressed him. "It says here you are a senior research worker – a person of federal standing. And you are taking such an irresponsible step as to buy a motorcycle!" My father was a computer scientist still writing his dissertation, but even a traffic policeman knew his work held value for the Soviet state.

But if toiling for the state held inflated meaning, then intellectual activity deemed in any way subversive would seem even more significant. At different times, a word written, a poem recited, a book owned could lead to grave consequences for the transgressor, from loss of social standing, to prison, to death. The more the Word was pushed underground, the more it became imbued with mythical, possibly lethal power.

The country first got a taste of that power in the late 1950s and early 1960s, during the period dubbed the Thaw, after a novel by Ilya Ehrenburg that was published a year after Stalin's death and, it seemed, ushered in a new, freer era. Some historians, including the great partnership of Mikhail Heller and Alexander Nekrich, believe that the Thaw was an unintentional side effect of Nikita Khrushchev's ruthless years-long power grab. Certainly, the freedoms of the Thaw were relative. Throughout the late 1950s people were persecuted, put on trial and imprisoned for what they said and wrote. In 1958 the world watched in horror as the Soviet government shepherded a mob that verbally trampled the poet Boris Pasternak, awarded the Nobel Prize for his novel *Doctor Zhivago* that year. Still, a certain reprieve from the paralyzing fear of the Stalin years, combined with some economic relief after the hungry postwar decade, produced an atmosphere that shaped one of the most important generations in Soviet history, the *shestidesiatniki,* or "sixties people."

They rediscovered the Word. They found it in poetry that had been concealed from them – the poetry of the turn of the century, the 1910s and 1920s, when poetry flourished in Russia as never before or since.

This is how Liudmila Alekseyeva, a chronicler of dissidence in the Soviet Union, describes this time:

> Moscow and Leningrad were literally flooded by copies of poems by banned, forgotten or repressed poets of the pre-Revolutionary and Soviet times – Akhmatova, Mandelstam, Voloshin, Gumilev, Tsvetaeva and many others preserved in the memory of people of an older generation. . . . A passion for poetry became a sign of the times. Poetry took over the hearts of people who had had no particular interest in poetry or in literature generally before and would have none later. Moreover, a heightened need for self-expression, awakened in a society that had come out of its paralysis, made many put pen to paper. [By one estimate] works by some 300 authors circulated in the samizdat of the time. Most of them were young.
>
> Vladimir Bukovsky [a young organizer of poetry readings arrested and forced into a psychiatric hospital] writes of that time that in offices and institutions all over Moscow typewriters were always in use and overuse: everyone who had the opportunity was typing – for himself and for friends – poems, poems, poems. There appeared a youth subculture in which the knowledge of poems by Pasternak, Mandelstam, Gumilev served as a password.

Who can tell now why it was poetry? Perhaps it had something to do with the fact that poetry is short and can be reproduced and distributed easily – the style of the time was to fold a sheet of paper in half and type on both sides, creating an ersatz book spread. But perhaps it was also that the young people of the time discovered in the poetic word a new and vital way of expressing their sensations and perceptions. The poetic word, in contrast to the prose of socialist realism, almost inevitably opens the door to numerous interpretations. This might explain the early samizdatchiks' utterly undiscriminating tastes. An issue of *Syntaxis*, a samizdat poetry journal, placed poems by the great masters of the past, such as Osip Mandelstam, alongside young geniuses like Joseph Brodsky and the likes of this: "Stigmata of revelations in the lie/Crawling atop live sculptures – /But what do I care, pray tell,/When I am an eternal wanderer in your love."

In the summer of 1958 a monument to Vladimir Mayakovsky was

unveiled in the center of Moscow. It quickly became a gathering place for young poetry lovers and the site of improvised readings. The authorities greeted the initiative enthusiastically at first but quickly grew disenchanted with its excessive free-spiritedness. A new KGB chief appointed at the end of 1958 launched an all-out campaign against the university and high-school students who took part in the gatherings. Historians Nekrich and Heller point out that the new security chief had an excellent humanities education and "could truly appreciate the significance of what was happening at Mayakovsky Square." The young people were chased away from the monument for a time. In May 1961 they returned for a reading devoted to the thirtieth anniversary of the poet's suicide. That evening the KGB orchestrated a mêlée that ended with the beating of many reading participants and the arrest of three of the organizers. They were tried and sentenced to long prison terms for "anti-Soviet propaganda."

Three years later came the arrest of the young Leningrad poet Joseph Brodsky. He was tried and sentenced to internal exile for "not working." The year 1965 saw the arrest of two writers, Andrei Siniavsky and Yuli Daniel, who had published their works abroad, as Pasternak had done before them. They were sentenced to five- and seven-year prison terms.

One after another, these arrests and trials signaled first the limits and then the end of the Thaw. The magical era ended as quickly as it had begun. But not before it had shaped the *shestidesiatniki* generation, given birth to samizdat – underground self-publishing – and reinvigorated the free word.

The Thaw shaped the post-World War II incarnation of the intelligentsia, a new generation beholden to the power of the Word and saddled with the burden of responsibility for the fate of the country. After the Thaw was over, some of the *shestidesiatniki*, like Larisa Bogoraz and Sergei Kovaliov, went on to form the dissident movement – rather, the small groups of like-minded courageous discontents that produced the illusion of ongoing organized activity. They lost their jobs, stood trial, went to prison and into internal exile, and by the late 1970s and early 1980s more and more of them were being forced to emigrate.

But the majority of those who read poetry in the squares during the Thaw retreated from the public sphere, going into a sort of hibernation. They chose contemplative careers as researchers or translators; less often they entered the more active, what the regime called "ideological," professions of writer, journalist or teacher. But privately, they continued to collect and reproduce words. Samizdat took on the measured, dependable pace of a long-term venture. As the students of the Thaw grew up, they bought their own East-German-made Eureka brand typewriters and produced home-made books, often complete with covers and illustrations.

In the early seventies samizdat was supplemented by *tamizdat*. If samizdat was literally translated as "self-publishing," then *tamizdat* meant "there-publishing," as in Russian-language books published abroad. The best-known source of *tamizdat* was the Ardis publishing house in the United States, a cottage operation launched in 1971 by a young professor and his graduate-student wife. For twenty years they smuggled pre-Revolutionary editions and contemporary manuscripts out of the Soviet Union, printed them and smuggled them back in. All in all, they published over 200 titles. Other *tamizdat* outlets, most of them organized by *émigrés*, added to the list. The precious books were passed around within small circles of friends. Their words became passwords; intelligentsia speech grew more and more heavily laced with quotations, each of which signified membership in a certain select group.

With the generation of the 1970s – those born in the 1950s – samizdat turned more and more inward. Those who started writing then hardly entertained much hope or desire to see their work published in their country. They wrote explicitly for themselves and their friends. Their language was insular, their work filled with friendly references and private jokes. Many of them chose not to seek careers but to find jobs that afforded them plenty of free time. They have been called "the generation of night guards and boiler-men" – these jobs were popular because they traditionally required working only one twenty-four-hour shift every four days.

"I have the honor – and I really mean the *honor*," wrote Sergei

Gandlevsky, an outstanding poet of that generation, "of belonging to a circle of writers who managed once and for all to bridle their desire to be printed. In Soviet media, anyway. . . . For us, literature was private business. The kitchen, the guard's booth and the boiler room could not accommodate the abstract reader, the people, the country. There was no one whose eyes were to be opened, who needed to be convinced. Everyone knew everything as it was. There was nothing there to produce a sense of civic duty as an impetus to outward activity. So if any one of us wrote anything anti-Soviet, it could only be because that was where his heart lay."

This group was no less obsessed with morality and the Word than its intelligentsia predecessors. In conversation Gandlevsky once described what he called "the honesty psychosis" from which he and his friends suffered in the 1970s. "We were constantly taking things apart into what's honest and what's not, like medieval priests struggling to figure out how many angels can dance on the head of a pin. To work is to participate, which is dishonest, but to work as a night-guard making 70 roubles a month – that seems honest because you can't make any less and we don't want to kill ourselves. When I finally got to make money translating, I thought it was honest because I was merely translating, but then I translated a propaganda poem from the Ossetian, and that was dishonest. [The poet and architect] Mikhail Aisenberg restored buildings, and that was honest, but if one of the temples he restored was used to deceive visiting foreigners, that was dishonest. And most of all, we had this weary attitude toward speech, as toward a person who had once been caught stealing. Sometimes it seemed like all words were discredited. At one point I developed a love for going to the hardware store because it was full of such good, honest words: *planer, secateurs, sawhorse*."

The relentless pursuit of a moral high ground was vintage intelligentsia. But for the seventies generation it was deeply personal, not profoundly public as in the case of their predecessors. The ultimate goal was to be and stay honorable. To be sure, all the wordly activities of the *shestidesiatniki* had, of necessity, a similar chamber quality. A singer-songwriter of that generation, Aleksandr Galich, used to sing, "My Eureka makes four copies./And that's all. And it's enough." The people who made up the convoluted samizdat and *tamizdat* distribution chains kept their involvement secret, often from their friends, usually from their children and sometimes even from their spouses.

As the daughter of a woman who had recited her verse at the Mayakovsky monument and, it seemed, spent her entire late teens and early twenties memorizing, typing and retyping poetry, I grew up surrounded by banned books. More to the point, I grew up *on* them – reading them and, of course, making them, complete with my rather helpless illustrations. As I got older, I saw more and more books published by Ardis, the little American house. My parents evaded questions about the source of the books.

Nearly two decades later, in 1996, having returned to live in my grandmother's Writers' Union flat, I saw a woman who had been our next-door neighbor. She had known me as a baby and instructed me in drawing when I was a teenager. She had long since emigrated to the United States but was back in town for a celebration – the twenty-fifth anniversary of Ardis. As it turned out, she had been the publishers' best friend and served as their main link to the Soviet Union: she had provided the rare editions from which they made facsimile books, and there surely was not an Ardis edition that had not gone through her apartment. Which was next door to ours. But this was information too explosive to entrust to a child – I had to wait nearly twenty years to learn it.

Certainly the palpable sense of danger kept the Thaw generation from performing the intelligentsia's most romanticized function: enlightening the masses. If fear stopped a *tamizdat* distributor from being open with a friend's child, who would even dream of going to the People? Still, despite the fear, despite the desperately closed quality of intellectual circles, the Thaw generation was not introverted like the younger group. Rather, they were lying low waiting for their golden hour. Whether it was the magical experience of their youth or their general love of romantic poetry, they somehow believed that the time would come for them to speak, and then a word of truth – and they had accumulated many words of truth – would change the country.

*

Miraculously, it happened. The freedom to speak – rather, the task of speaking – was handed down in the late 1980s by a party apparatchik apparently infatuated with the intelligentsia. Mikhail Gorbachev had been the first person in his southern Russia village to be accepted at Moscow State University. As a boy, he had idolized Vissarion Belinsky, a great Russian literary critic and an icon of nineteenth-century intelligentsia. Gorbachev was a student in Moscow at the start of the Thaw. He was married to a scholar. His language was a bizarre mix of intellectualisms and party demagoguery – a striking departure from his predecessors, who had specialized in impenetrable "apparatese."

It seems Gorbachev wanted to use the media to help shake the country up, whip it into shape. He appeared to think the process of opening the flow of information could be orchestrated from the top. Though he virtually abolished censorship in 1988, under his leadership the Central Committee of the Party continued to appoint the editors of national publications and monitor and influence their content. In his memoirs, published in 1995, Gorbachev bemoaned the fact that "glasnost broke out of the framework that had initially been set for it and turned into a process independent of anyone's decrees or directives."

A child of the party machine – he was drafted into party work right after college – Gorbachev had admired the word-hoarding intelligentsia from afar. He had little idea of the force he would unleash. The *shestidesiatniki* broke out of their cocoon and rushed to force open the floodgates of words. From about 1987 until roughly 1991 major Soviet publications printed a nearly complete collection of samizdat and *tamizdat*; it was no accident that most of them were headed by people who came of age during the Thaw.

The press runs of major publications skyrocketed. At the height of glasnost so-called "thick journals" – literary journals that had always been the province of a professional elite – hit a circulation of five million. People passed around the latest issues of the journals and other flagship perestroika publications. They cut out novels that were printed in installments and had them bound into custom-made books. Discussions of the un-banned publications raged not only in kitchens but on public transport and at the beach. The Word had broken loose, and with it ideas began to rage. Writers entered into earnest and urgent debates on the proper role of the individual in society, the necessary weight of the law, the best social structure in which to live. In a society taught never to question anything, everything now seemed fair game. With hierarchies toppling in every area, a single well-argued article could make a scholar, writer or inspired amateur instantly famous. The intelligentsia in all its incarnations had always dreamed of a debate so vital as to envelop the country.

Most amazing, the discussion went far beyond the confines of professional clubs and research institutes to move the people that the intelligentsia deeply suspected were the People. These people not only comprised the astronomical journal circulation figures but came out by the hundred thousand to take part in rallies. They chanted "Down with the Party!" at the height of a debate about the Party's pre-eminence in the government. They shouted words of democracy, hope and support for Yeltsin in March 1991, when Gorbachev, in his last desperate attempt to moderate the changes, banned public demonstrations in Moscow but the people came out anyway. And they came out during the August 1991 coup to form a protective ring around the Moscow White House, where Yeltsin sat symbolizing a bright democratic future.

Then the People went home. The press runs fell as drastically as they had risen. The rallies stopped. The protests quieted down. The high of glasnost and perestroika was followed by a brief plateau of self-satisfaction followed by a nightmare of inflation, destruction, depression, bureaucratic battles, aggressive alienation, a morbid festering national identity crisis and frightening, impenetrable apathy.

The intelligentsia was again alone, an island of torment wedged between the newly entrenched government and the once-again indifferent People. The revolution wrought by the Word, it turned out, was either an illusion or reversible: either way, it was no revolution at all. In all likelihood, the rush on information was largely a result of something the regime and the intelligentsia had, not very consciously, been cooperating on for years: inflating the worth of words. Even approved publications had been carefully rationed: subscriptions to intellectual publications like the weekly *Literaturnaya gazeta* were hard to get. Samizdat and *tamizdat* were all the sweeter for being forbidden fruit. But for many people a brief taste was enough to satisfy their curiosity. To others, tomes of gruesome memories and heavy ideas seemed repetitive.

In every way the intelligentsia was left alone with its devalued treasures. The research institutes that had so recently seemed eternal started collapsing one after another: the government cut funding for all scholarship. The publishing houses, also left without customary budgetary infusions, began closing or, attempting to adjust to the new marketplace, asking writers to pay for the printing of their own books. The old systems of perks for writers, artists, architects and others dwindled. The intelligentsia stood stripped of its money, its prestige and its faith.

Everything that had always been no longer was. The Word was cheap, the Truth as unknowable as the People.

In addition, the intelligentsia, seemingly homogeneous for so long, turned out to have been united merely by its opposition to the regime. During the glasnost era this unity first showed cracks, dividing the intelligentsia into the Westernists and the Slavophiles, the atheists and the religious, the liberals and the monarchists. These ideological divides were as old as the phenomenon of the intelligentsia itself but for several decades they had been concealed. Certainly there was not much new or unique to Russia in the social forces that started to split the intelligentsia into those who made money and those who did not, those who changed professions and adapted to new conditions and those who proudly eked out a familiar shoestring existence. Finally, nothing was novel in the rush to declare the intelligentsia dead once and for all. For example, two prominent Russian scholars, Boris Dubin and Lev Gudkov, praised the demise of what they dubbed "literary political delusions" and promised that soon Russia would rid itself of the dysfunctional intelligentsia in favor of a productive class of intellectual professionals.

I have either more faith in this tradition or less faith in change. Certainly as long as bearded men in war zones reproach their countrymen for not heeding the words of Dostoyevsky, the intelligentsia is alive in

Russia. Still, it is engaged, as is its way, in a massive, desperate search. It is seeking its place in the new Russian society. And it is seeking truths to replace the faith that saw it to perestroika.

Here I have attempted to document this search. Most of the people in this book came of age in the 1960s and 1970s. They are scholars, writers and night-guards. Possibly a majority of them are poets. All of them are looking for ways to make themselves feel useful and important. Some of the paths they choose are, to me, ugly and frightening; others appear born of desperation and helplessness; still others, in the best intelligentsia traditions, are as inspiring as they are hopeless.

PART TWO

THE SEARCH FOR TRUTH

CHAPTER ONE

THE DOOM-SAYERS

Time stood still in the Soviet Union of the 1970s and early 1980s. Later this era would be dubbed the Stagnation Period, a rather dismissive designation for the first segment of twentieth-century Russian history that was marked by no major internal upheavals, no purges and no revelations, no revolutions and no wars on Soviet territory, just the steady spectacle of the country's leaders growing ever older. But then it was also a time of great, unparalleled faith. We knew things would always be just as they were. We the children of the Eastern Bloc sang the same song, a simple tune that well after the fall of Communism continued to serve as a password among people who grew up in this region:

> Let there always be sky,
> Let there always be sun,
> Let there always be mama,
> Let there always be me.

This ditty defined the magnitude of stability we knew to expect of life. People would hold the same jobs for decades, probably for their entire lives. We would grow up and grow old not only in the same country ruled by the same leaders but, in all likelihood, in the same neighborhood and even the same apartment, seeing the same people, reading the same books and thinking the same thoughts. In a region of the world that was shaped entirely by the twentieth century's two bloodiest wars, not only catastrophe but mere change had been ruled out of bounds.

If in Stalin's time and even during the Thaw the worst sin one could commit was saying that the Soviet system was not the best in the world, then by the 1970s the most grievous heresy was to imply that the Soviet regime would not exist eternally. Even among the dissidents only a few dared advance this idea. The writer Andrei Amalrik wrote a short book entitled *Will the Soviet Union Last until 1984?* He was convinced the country would succumb to a Chinese invasion. A matriarch of Russian writers, Lydia Chukovskaya, predicted that Moscow would one day boast an Aleksandr Solzhenitsyn Square and an Andrei Sakharov Avenue. But such prophecies were presented and heard as rhetoric. The logic of the time proved over and over again that this time would never end.

The mortal nature of the regime remained taboo well into the glasnost era. In 1987 an outstanding journalist, Vasily Seliunin, published an article titled "The Devious Number," in which he presented the results of a five-year study he had undertaken together with an economist friend. The Soviet economy was a house of cards, they argued, propped up by statistics calculated out of thin air. The article went down in the history of perestroika as a major journalistic milestone, but half of it had been censored out – the part in which the authors argued that the Soviet Union was nearing its demise.

The Soviet Union had to die its sudden, incomprehensible death before we finally believed that it was mortal. But the entire perestroika era felt like a death agony. It began on April 26, 1986, with the explosion of one of the Chernobyl nuclear power plant reactors. Four months later a prominent writer, Yury Nagibin, recorded in his journal: "The entire country is falling out Chernobyl-like. Matter is disintegrating uncontrollably, and spiritual substance is dissipating." No matter what the authorities then did to stem the leaks of radiation and information, the country grew sick with the devastating news, which stripped it of its faith and its future.

After Chernobyl, catastrophe became a national obsession. Starting around 1990, once apocalyptic predictions were allowed to see print, the media brimmed with descriptions of the impending end of the world or at least the Russian nation. A number of morbid clichés vied for the status of common knowledge. One theory held it that falling birth rates spelled the imminent demise of the Russian people, which numbered about 150 million. Another argued quite convincingly that the Chernobyl accident was a harbinger of nuclear catastrophes still to come. A slew of others warned about the deathly threats that AIDS, rock music, capitalism, Communism, young people and the aging of the population posed to the future of the land and the rest of the world.

Some pundits became professional doom-sayers. Following his return to Russia in 1994 Aleksandr Solzhenitsyn acquired a weekly television show. Every Monday for about a year he broadcast his scenario of the end of Russia. It was an eerie spectacle. Solzhenitsyn, who had spent about half of his life cut off from live communication in Russian with more than a couple of people – he had spent eight years in labor camps, four in internal exile, and twenty reclusive years in exile abroad – sounded as if his voice came from a different world, one in which words had been sealed off and were just now being allowed to escape with a current of stale air, which distorted their sound. He had spent decades studying the Russian language that preceded the twentieth century, so his speech carried an unfamiliar tinge. His movements were jerky, his stare – well, crazed.

He chose a different topic for each of his weekly sermons – the crisis in education, the destructive presence of foreigners in Russia, the poor physical health of Russian youth – but the leitmotif was the looming threat to Russians as an ethnic group. "I've already had to speak about the extinction of the people," he would say toward the end of the program and, with a dismissive gesture, cite birth-rate statistics: in the mid-1990s Russian women were having an average of fewer than two babies each, while in 1875, according to his figures, each woman had given birth seven times.

In a book-length essay published in 1995 Solzhenitsyn defined the current state of affairs as "The Great Russian Catastrophe of the nineties of the twentieth century." He wrote:

> The Catastrophe comprises, first of all, our extinction. And our losses shall grow: in today's unremitting poverty, how many women will summon the courage to give birth? No lesser a part of the Catastrophe are retarded and ill children, and these multiply because of the living conditions and the boundless drinking of their fathers. And the complete failure of our schools, incapable today of rearing a generation that would be informed

and morally upstanding. And a shortage of living space that places us far behind the civilized world. And the swarming of bribe-takers in the state apparatus, including those who cheaply sell off our oil and rare metals to foreign markets. . . . And the Catastrophe is in the division of Russians, as though into two different peoples: a giant provincial and rural mass and, utterly unlike it, a small number of capital dwellers imbued with Western culture. The Catastrophe is in today's amorphous nature of the Russian national consciousness, in a gray indifference to our national affiliation and an even greater indifference to compatriots in trouble. And the Catastrophe is in the handicaps inflicted upon our intellect by the Soviet era: the lies of Communism have been so layered upon consciousness that many do not even recognize they have blinkers on their eyes. And the Catastrophe is that we have too few people who could become state leaders who would be at once wise, courageous and selfless.

In all, nine apocalyptic conditions. Most of these, certainly, were Solzhenitsyn's personal observations. As for his interpretation of statistics, it was rather flawed: there was no real indication that the Russian nation, one of the world's most numerous, was on the verge of extinction; the falling birth rate and shifting age demographics matched those of most of the post-World War II countries. Still, this prediction of imminent national demise became a cornerstone of the new genre of doom-saying. Solzhenitsyn was the undisputed leader in this field, but other nationalist-minded thinkers put in a steady stream of their own contributions.

In 1994 Nikolai Ryzhkov, the Gorbachev-era prime minister, founded the Moscow Intellectual and Business Club, whose monthly meetings turned into verbal competitions in apocalyptic theorizing. At a November 1994 meeting one participant, Cossack chieftain Aleksandr Martynov, predicted that "entire Chinese divisions can easily cross the Amur river and encounter no obstacles in penetrating the depths of Siberia and the Far East for many, many hundreds of kilometers." Yelena Panina, the chairwoman of the Russian Zemstvo Movement, declared that 70–80 percent of Russia's wealth was being bought up by foreign firms acting undercover. Another contributor, the mathematician Nikita Moiseyev, opined, "We are living on the edge of a knife. One careless move – and we fall into the abyss of the Latin-American comprador route of

Côte d'Azur

development, when the nation sinks further and further into poverty while its assets are transformed into the real estate of the Azure Shores."

Nikita Moiseyev, by then well into his seventies, was a unique figure in the emerging field of apocalyptic thought. Once a leading Soviet mathematician, a member of the exclusive Academy of Sciences, the chairman of the Moscow House of the Scholars, a fixture of intelligentsia gatherings for decades, he had spent the last twenty years specializing in predicting apocalypses. In the 1970s he modeled nuclear winter – the deep freeze that would follow nuclear catastrophe. At the height of the arms race, this was revolutionary research, which Moiseyev was not allowed to leave the country to present. Furthermore, when a co-author of his went to Spain to report their results at a conference, this scientist vanished without a trace; naturally, scholarly lore credited the KGB with his disappearance. In the 1990s Moiseyev headed up the Council on the Analysis of Critical Situations, a governmental body apparently created especially for him. He was now busy modeling the end of the world, caused by overpopulation and destruction of the environment.

Moiseyev, once known for his nonconformist views – which passed for liberalism – joined the ranks of those he himself dubbed "patriotic scholars," a growing group of intellectuals who seemed genuinely frightened by the end of the country as they knew it. He advocated creating a new mammothly ambitious development program akin to the GOELRO plan, drafted in 1920 by a group of 200 scientists and engineers appointed by Lenin himself and known as the State Committee on the Electrification of Russia. The GOELRO slogan, "Communism equals the power of the Soviets plus the electrification of the entire country," adorned Moscow's Mayakovsky Square right through perestroika, not so much setting a goal as affirming the faith in the Soviet Union as a great and powerful country – a faith founded in a vague awareness of technological progress and lofty goals.

Now, argued Moiseyev, "if you speak with the people, you will find a most outrageous sense of hopelessness." He offered a contrasting memory from his childhood: "I come from a family of engineers. I remember how, in the mid-1920s, my grandfather and his colleagues, old engineers whose thinking was far from pro-Soviet, received the GOELRO plan.

Returning from a trip to [the town of] Kashira, where a power station was under construction, my grandfather said roughly the following to my father: 'Listen, it looks like the Bolsheviks really do want to revitalize Russia.' . . . Today we need something like the GOELRO plan. We need to envision a future. Such a program could stimulate the development of that condition of the people that Lenin termed 'a breakthrough.' Furthermore, without such a plan it will be impossible to break out of the current catastrophe."

The sense of doom that pervaded the country after eternal institutions proved mortal lent itself best to the sorts of nationalist rhetoric advanced by Solzhenitsyn and the Ryzhkov crowd. The language of liberals does not accommodate the fear of extinction quite as well. Still, the liberal, Westernist intelligentsia was staring into an abyss no less frightening. It was finding itself profoundly alone in its own country and in the world; it seemed it had outlived its usefulness.

"My books used to have press runs of 200,000 copies, and still the next day they would be gone from the stores," Leonid Zhukhovitsky, one of my neighbors in the Writers' Union building, recalled wistfully. "I knew who I was writing for. I received up to 30,000 letters a year. Today I can write and print whatever I feel like. If I don't proofread the galleys myself, they will even preserve all my typos. But to be honest, I do not know who I write for anymore. The press runs are very small. It is difficult for me today to envision a piece of writing that the entire country would talk about, as it used to happen. . . . We used to be the philosophers, the economists and all but ministers. People used to come to writers with all their problems. Now, thank God, we have philosophers, sociologists, political scientists, economists, lawyers and all sorts of professionals. But it has been bad for literature. It has now assumed the same modest place as it holds in the entire civilized world."

Zhukhovitsky was among the most prominent *shestidesiatniki*, the generation of the Thaw. He belonged to that universal category of writers that prop up the publishing industry in any country in the world: he produced wholesome but engaging love stories at the rate of about a book a year. He was a similarly prolific playwright. He was also a journalist – indeed, a large number of people who entered journalism in the seventies and eighties considered him their mentor. Early on in his writing career, Zhukhovitsky advanced the private theory of "living beside the system," as he put it. "At one point I had to decide what I was calling upon my readers to do, for a good part of writing is a sermon. I could not call upon people to battle the regime, because the regime would simply stomp you into the dirt without noticing; I couldn't tell people to live in concert with the regime – people would lose their souls, stop being human. So I devised this formula: one had to live beside the system. One had to be a friend, one had to love, read, create, travel, claim all the living space that the system had not yet hidden behind barbed wire – and one had to try to broaden that space in every way. I tried to – please forgive this word – *rear* a person who was capable of happiness. And I think that when there had matured several generations of people who felt free in love and friendship, for millions of people the system started to take up less and less space in life. Perhaps that's why it collapsed so easily."

Zhukhovitsky was that rare theorist who practiced what he preached. He never joined the Party, but he dabbled in protest-letter writing when he felt moved. He never took a staff job, and he proudly maintained the reputation of a lech. His unparalleled consistency allowed him to carve out a niche of trust within Soviet journalism, which he managed to use not only to communicate (a feat in itself) but to make social change. In the 1970s he scored two monumental victories. An article entitled "The Invalid" in *Literaturnaya gazeta* told the stories of people disabled by World War II injuries and precipitated legal measures that provided a set of special benefits for this group. In 1974 Zhukhovitsky printed a story called "Love and Demography," in which he railed against the hypocrisy of a nation that fretted over low birth rates but stigmatized single mothers. Zhukhovitsky credited himself with changing attitudes toward single motherhood, and he was not exaggerating all that much.

"But that was at a time when newspapers had press runs of five, six, fifteen, twenty, twenty-five million, and a single article could play this sort of role," he sighed. For years he had been wishing he could gather an audience of this scale again. Since the late 1980s he had been trying to alert the world to a crisis that threatened to destroy it. He called it the "crisis of global morality."

"For a long time I have not only noticed but have been touched, angered and outraged by the low, base nature of world relations today." He leaned back slightly in a rocking chair in his sunny office furnished with books and antique bent-wood furniture. "A number of principles that are considered noble are, in reality, not only immoral but actually low. For example, the principle of non-intervention, the principle of sovereignty – these principles are absolutely antihuman. I was once speaking with a good friend, a Swedish writer, about Swedish neutrality. And suddenly it occurred to me to ask, 'What about during the war? Your neighbors were conquered, annihilated and so on. And you were just standing off to the side – that's the same as not to help a person who has been attacked by bandits.' We have always thought that neutrality is noble. But in reality, in human terms, it is shameful."

There was a delicious view of the West that flourished in the Soviet Union in the 1970s and 1980s. For most people, including Zhukhovitsky, the West as a geographic destination was as inaccessible as Mars. But messages from the West sustained them. These were Agatha Christie and John Le Carré novels, Russian-language broadcasts by the Voice of America, the BBC Russian Service and Radio Free Europe. And, of course, these were Russian books published abroad and occasional earnest words of support from the odd visiting foreigner who saw his Russian friends as valiantly struggling for liberty. There emerged a composite portrait of the West not only as a bastion of freedom but as a benevolent and endlessly wise parent – or at least a friendly police officer.

In the late eighties, when Russians outside the party elite were granted the right to travel freely, the intelligentsia rushed to meet the West on what was probably one of the most tragic blind dates in history. The West disappointed bitterly. "I understood that we cannot rely on the West," said Zhukhovitsky. "When I went to America during the Gorbachev era, I attempted to explain to my listeners that it was necessary to help Russian democracy. They often objected with something like, 'Why do we have to help you?' I had to explain that this was not at all the way it was – it was *us* helping *them*, because we here were fighting for their survival. In the early thirties people used to ask, 'Why should England and France help German antifascists?' So they didn't. And they didn't help themselves. And the Americans refused to understand that even if, say, Rwanda or Somalia has no nuclear weapons and does not threaten anyone, famine in Rwanda is still a direct threat to full-tummied America. Because Americans who close their eyes to the famine in Rwanda become socially dangerous in their own country. A person whose conscience atrophies becomes a threat to his fellow citizens. If it is not frightening to see the death of people in Rwanda, it will not be frightening to see the death of people in Texas, and if it's not frightening to see death, then it's not so frightening to kill."

Zhukhovitsky was not affecting schoolgirlish naïveté; he was speaking from a belief in the moral goodness of the West that had been formed over decades. The moral line Zhukhovitsky was attempting to teach was in fact what he had expected to see when he traveled abroad and met the people who once smuggled protest letters out of the Soviet Union. Dostoyevsky wrote that "beauty will save the world." The Soviet-era intelligentsia was convinced that salvation lay in moral goodness. When he found no such thing as a morally upstanding or even a morally concerned nation, Zhukhovitsky drew the reasonable conclusion that the world was coming to an end.

The prolific Zhukhovitsky unleashed a torrent of articles and think-papers and, in 1989, even organized an international conference on "global morals." The cream of the Russian intelligentsia, including those living in foreign exile, presented their views on the state of the world's moral fabric. But, said Zhukhovitsky ruefully, "It was an odd thing. The idea itself ignited people. But because I am no organizer, it all came to nothing. I had hoped that some sort of mechanism would come into action and either the United Nations or someone else would take on the issue." That is how it had worked in Soviet times: the dissidents would identify a problem, find a way to communicate it to the West, and often see their demands introduced in high-level international negotiations. This had worked with the issue of Jews attempting to leave the country: in the early 1970s the first protest letters on this issue appeared; by the end of the decade the United States President was demanding that Jews be granted the right to emigrate as a condition for negotiations. Naturally, it seemed that one had only to articulate an issue in order for the world's powerful institutions to address it.

There was no question that Zhukhovitsky had focused on a dire problem. "There are a number of threats hanging over humanity," he argued, "but because there are no global moral standards, everything is decided in a particular country by a particular government, which may be democratic or fascistic. Only when something tragic finally happens does the so-called international community intervene, as it did in Iraq. Take, for example, the threat of terrorism. Terrorists have only to attain nuclear weapons – and at this point that's not so difficult, since they can be manufactured virtually at the home-workshop level. And there are a number of other threats, such as new epidemics."

Zhukhovitsky envisioned some sort of a global moral police force that would intervene in all cases of human rights violations, punishing the perpetrators among state leaders and repairing the damaged society. Better yet, he thought, the world could act preventively, for example to avert the return of Communism in Russia. Speaking with me the day after the July 1996 presidential election, in which Boris Yeltsin beat his Communist challenger in a frightfully close race, Zhukhovitsky projected fatigued disappointment. "We are lucky that yesterday we slipped by and Russia remained democratic. But for five years there has been this sense that Russian affairs are just ours. And what if we had not managed this situation? The international community would have had to spend relatively little to ensure a better standard of living in Russia so that people would not vote for the Communists, and the world did not want to do it. But if, God forbid, the Communists had attained power, it would have cost the world hundreds of billions of dollars for defense. And the issue would not have been just the threat of nuclear attack – the chaos in Russia would no doubt have led to several accidents at nuclear power plants."

If the Soviet system could be dismantled, then certainly the existing system of world relations could be changed; all that was required was a public understanding of the inadequacy of the world's existing operating principles. Zhukhovitsky's logic was impeccable, and his disappointment all the more helplessly bitter for that. By the time he traveled to the United States for his second lecture tour, in 1992, he was resorting to shock tactics. "I began by saying that I could guarantee that Russia would last another eleven months. There was no response. So I began the next lecture differently: I said that I could guarantee that America would last another eleven months and one week. The reaction was entirely different: general interest, people all but jumping up off their seats. 'Why?' 'What?' 'How?' I explained that Russia would last another eleven months because we had sufficient food supplies for that amount of time – and that famine in Russia would spell the end of America. They asked, 'Could Russia start nuclear war?' I had to explain to them that we have different traditions, a different mentality. There would be hundreds of officers in the country whose children had died of hunger and who would not think twice before launching rockets with hydrogen bombs toward America. Because in our tradition, if a house catches on fire, then the entire village runs to put out the fire. If someone does not come, then the last piece of smoldering wood flies toward his house. Those are the rules."

Not long after Zhukhovitsky took to frightening American students, Russia's foreign minister, Andrei Kozyrev, attempted the same scare tactics with the international diplomatic community. In 1993 on the floor of the United Nations he gave a militant speech intended to shock his listeners into recalling the fear to which the Soviet Union had subjected the Cold War world. Kozyrev was a product of a very similar liberal-intelligentsia environment to Zhukhovitsky's. A diplomat whose job it was to gain the world's attention, he apparently perceived the same indifference among his international colleagues as Zhukhovitsky saw in his foreign students. Then again, perhaps it was something else. The further the emotional and mental high of perestroika receded into the past, the vaster and more indifferent the world that opened up before these two men and many others, the greater the fear that gripped them. Like many lonely and mortal men before them, they sought the incomparable comfort of words of the strength and righteousness of aggressive nationalism.

Their aggression was like that of a cheated lover – impulsive at first, the spark of anger striking affection, then gradually giving way to a genuine dislike, a defensive self-sufficiency. Zhukhovitsky, like many others, had been betrayed. And every betrayal is certainly the end of a private world.

Russia after the fall of Communism was populated by men and women whose ideals, hopes and even ordinary plans had been betrayed. Some, like Zhukhovitsky, had lost the idol they had made of the West. Others, like, perhaps, Nikita Moiseyev, had lost the sense of purpose and common cause that had once sustained them. Whatever unassailable certainty had made life worth living, it had slipped, shattered or shown its ugly flip side. No wonder it seemed like the world was ending.

CHAPTER TWO

THE GENIUS JEW-HATER

The truth is, I had to lie to interview him. At first I tried to be upfront about it. In the winter of 1995 at Moscow's opulent House of the Scholars, a place where the intelligentsia comes to revel in being the intelligentsia, I approached Igor Shafarevich following the première of his new film, a sort of cinelecture on Russian history. I said I wanted to interview him for an American magazine. From his very impressive height, Shafarevich looked down his nose at mine. Mine, in the extensive Russian vocabulary of ethnic signifiers, screams "Jewish." He said no interview, ever. To end the conversation, he lumbered off the stage and literally ran down the chandelier-lit hall.

Over the preceding five years Doctor Shafarevich, a mathematician cum political philosopher, had spent much time denying that he was an anti-Semite. Giving him the benefit of the doubt, I asked a colleague to call and ask to interview him for a German magazine. Shafarevich cheerily invited her to his home. I wrote down all my questions, prepped the lucky interviewer, and went along posing as the photographer.

Of course, I reasoned, he could be just anti-American. Either way, he was a man of his time. Rather, at seventy-one, having lived through several distinct epochs in the history of his country, he was a man of his many times. What seemed uncanny was his relationship to his eras: in every period he had stood at the intellectual forefront of an important social trend. He had been a precocious scholar in the 1950s, a dissident in the 1970s, and a nationalist in the 1990s. In every incarnation he reached sufficient prominence to become not merely a product but a symbol of his time. In the mid-1990s he had once again positioned himself as an authority in an influential school of thought: the ultranationalist philosophy that was spreading steadily leftward of the far right honored him as its guru.

His first larger-than-life-size appearance came in 1940, when, at the tender age of sixteen, he was already a senior at Moscow State University and a recipient of the highest scholarly honor – the Stalin Stipend. A propaganda film made that year broadcast the images of a laborer, a collective farmer and "Shafarevich, a student" as examples for the country to follow. Shafarevich was a perfect specimen of the new Soviet intellectual, a brave new scholar of the first post-Revolutionary generation. Tall and athletic, with a stubble-covered round head, he was the robust blue-eyed opposite of the egg-headed bookworm; he was filmed cross-country skiing.

Mathematics was a good choice for one young, gifted and Soviet. Scholarship in the humanities was dictated from the top, and not even the slightest misstep was required to lose one's freedom or even life. The exact sciences fared partly better: biology was destroyed in the name of Lysenko, physics sustained decimating purges in the 1930s but was ultimately spared for the sake of the H-bomb, while mathematics – at once abstract, cheap and prestigious – was allowed to flourish. As Russian mathematician Askold Sossinsky has written, "Mathematics remained independent and pure: a theorem, once proved, was true, whether the party bosses liked it or not. Actually, until the end of the 1960s, the party bosses didn't particularly care, not only about theorems, but also about the people proving them."

A special place was reserved for young Shafarevich in the blessedly insular world of Soviet math. He was a protégé of two of the discipline's leading authorities, algebraists Ivan Vinogradov and Lev Pontriagin, who nudged him toward algebraic geometry, an emerging field in which Shafarevich would in short order become a world-class scholar. At the age of twenty-three, Shafarevich joined the faculty at the university, where he would teach for over twenty-five years, until he was banned from instruction. When he was thirty-four, he was elected to the Soviet Academy of Sciences, becoming the second-youngest member inducted in the twentieth century; the youngest was the physicist Andrei Sakharov. The same year, 1960, he was appointed head of the Algebra Department of the Steklov Institute, the world-famous center of Soviet mathematical thought, then headed by Vinogradov. His work on numbers theory was translated into a dozen languages.

Most of Shafarevich's staggering ascent no doubt stemmed from his remarkable talent; part of his career success was ensured by the high profile of his field of expertise; but the rest can be explained by the fact that, in the subtler subtopography of the mathematical establishment, Shafarevich from the beginning belonged to the more official group. His two mentors were known as conservatives and anti-Semites. In explaining the nature of Shafarevich's views, Yury Nagibin, a Jewish-identified Russian writer and a one-time acquaintance of the mathematician, wrote, "He was a student of . . . Pontriagin, a zoological anti-Semite who had in turn had the instruction of Academy Member Vinogradov, the father of the new school of mathematics and the grandfather of new anti-Semitism."

Over the decades of Shafarevich's prominence as a working mathematician, anti-Semitism was integral to staying power in the mathematics establishment. The first wave of anti-Semitic purges hit between 1946 and 1955, when Jews – the scapegoats of choice in a country devastated by the war – were systematically forced out of academe. Jewish university graduates were effectively barred from postgraduate study; practicing scholars found their efforts blocked, their studies discredited. This period, when the pool of talented young scholars suddenly shrank because the Jews were excluded, coincided with Shafarevich's steepest rise. The second period marked by anti-Semitic exclusion, from 1969 until 1989, when not a single Jew was hired by the Mechanics and Mathematics Department of Moscow State or by the Steklov Institute, occurred when Shafarevich was already well-established; that is, he fit in well with the approved mathematical establishment, which for decades was personified by Vinogradov.

Oddly, the repressive atmosphere that reigned in Soviet mathematics did little, if any, damage to the unique standing of great authority reserved for exact scientists in Soviet society. Sossinsky sums it up this way: "The long-standing prestige of the scientific profession in Russia amalgamat[es] the oriental reverence for the guru with the German respect for their Herr Professor and, at the same time, the traditional admiration for the self-denying and often naive efforts of the best citizens, aristocrats or intellectuals, to promote social justice by 'going to the people' and sharing their cultural legacy with the masses."

For a time, exact scientists of Shafarevich's generation, ensconced in their non-ideologized haven, manifested none of the traits of the self-sacrificing intelligentsia. Not that they could, during Stalin's reign: the best they could manage was to protect the unique intellectual atmosphere of the Russian mathematics community – and in time this environment would give fruit. The dissident movement was, one could argue, born in Moscow on December 5, 1965, and the impetus came from the mathematics community. Following the arrest of writers Andrei Siniavsky and Yuli Daniel, as many as 200 people gathered in Pushkin Square in Moscow for the first unsanctioned demonstration of the Soviet period. The organizer of the protest was Aleksandr Yesenin-Volpin, a mathematician and poet and a friend of Shafarevich.

The role of the exact scientist in fomenting dissent was consistent. The two spiritual leaders of the differently minded, Andrei Sakharov and Aleksandr Solzhenitsyn, were a physicist and a mathematician, respectively. Few statistics are available on the makeup of the dissident communities, but a breakdown done by the writer Andrei Amalrik in 1968 shows that 45 percent of those who signed protest letters then were exact scientists. One such letter, signed by ninety-nine mathematics professors at Moscow State following the arrest of Yesenin-Volpin for his incessant organizing activity, had devastating consequences for the mathematics community. The letter forced the state finally to realize that no intellectual activity should be left ideologically unmonitored. By order of the Central Committee of the Communist Party, the Mechanics and Mathematics Department of Moscow State – where Shafarevich was, by this time, one of the two most popular instructors – instituted new admissions and hiring policies, aimed at excluding Jews and free-thinkers of all stripes.

Twenty years later, when the US National Academy of Sciences tried to wrestle a resignation from Shafarevich, who had been nominated to the Academy by Sakharov, US scholars accused him of anti-Semitism and used the absence of Jews from his department at the Steklov Institute as proof (not that the rest of the Institute had hired any). But at the time, when the gap between party-line and dissenting mathematicians grew drastically wider, Shafarevich clearly positioned himself among the liberals. Being the most established and best-known mathematician on this side of the barricades, he quickly emerged as one of the most prominent dissenters. Every time Shafarevich appended his signature to a protest letter, short-wave radio stations such as Voice of America or Radio Free Europe, which were becoming the leading sources of information for the differently minded, highlighted his participation.

How did this star of Soviet scholarship become a human rights activist? Shafarevich seemed to have drifted into the role. His memory of his first dissident action was vague. "Yesenin-Volpin was a mathematician by education, that's why I knew him," he said, struggling to recover the memory. "This was fifteen years, I think, after Stalin's death, and he applied for a permit to hold a demonstration to commemorate this. As a response, he was committed to a nuthouse. He was, of course, a fairly odd person. But that is no basis for — mathematicians are almost all strange." As though to illustrate his point, Shafarevich directed his icy-blue stare at the supernaturally large slipper dangling precariously off the big toe of his right foot. Strange indeed.

He signed the letter in defense of Yesenin-Volpin and a few years later, another one: in defense of Sakharov, who had become the target of a vicious media campaign. Just signing those two letters was enough to position Shafarerich as a dissident, a member of a community just then taking shape. Shafarevich met Sakharov as a consequence of signing the second letter and soon joined the Committee for Human Rights in the USSR, organized in 1970 by Sakharov and two other physicists.

The committee, whose members banked on their fame — they hoped that it would keep them out of jail — was the first independent social-change organization in the Soviet Union. The activists intended to offer consultative help to the authorities in the area of human rights, but, since the authorities did not desire such help, the group concentrated on studying and documenting human rights abuses in the country.

Shafarevich found this state of affairs intensely frustrating. "It was not a very effective group," he shrugged dismissively. "It was always a reaction to what was happening." This criticism could be generalized to the entire dissident movement, which was born as a desperate scream to protest the clamping down on thought and speech that followed the brief Thaw, and continued as a sequence of letters, appeals, arrests and more letters. There were a few groups, some books and even a newspaper, but none of this added up to a movement. The movement that was not a movement had no unifying ideology: it loosely linked, rather than united, reform-minded Communists, right-leaning religious activists, and Westernizing free-speech fanatics. Nor did the dissident movement have a program or even a particular goal larger than to struggle against individual human rights abuses as they occurred.

The shortcomings of the dissidents as a group did not become apparent until twenty years later, when former dissidents joined the rest of the country in staring blankly into the enormous void left by the debunking of the official ideology. But in the early 1970s the lack of cohesion within the dissenting group was the key to its existence: there were too few people willing to risk their social status and even their freedom to draw ideological distinctions among them.

But Shafarevich longed for the grand idea, a sense of belonging to something extraordinary and extraordinarily large. In the nineties he derided his former colleagues for having committed the cardinal sin of the intelligentsia by failing to respond to the concerns of the People. "If someone was arrested, then there were letters of protest written about that," Shafarevich recalled with distaste. "Then the people who wrote the letters were also arrested. And it seemed that if they stopped arresting, they would stop writing letters, and if they stopped writing, they would stop arresting. One fed off the other. But from the point of view of the people, the general population, all this created a terrible impression." The community of people who purported to be fighting for human rights for all their countrymen was so small and closed, and the scope of issues that occupied them so narrow, in Shafarevich's view, that the mythical People had no use for such advocates.

Some prominent former dissidents clear on the opposite side of the political spectrum from Shafarevich have made similar statements, admitting, for example, that the dissidents focused on freedom of speech and the right to emigrate at the expense of pressing domestic economic and social issues, and the failure to address them has now come back to haunt them. "All this began," Shafarevich added, driving his damning point home, "back when collective farm workers did not have passports and could not move to the neighboring region. So from the people's point of view it seemed like a mockery to be fighting for the right to emigrate, as though the peasants' problems had been so insignificant that they were not people, did not exist. This, of course, repelled the people, and was the reason for the complete failure of the dissident movement. It failed completely."

Real dissidence, for Shafarevich, did not involve a provisional defense of human dignity against the state. It required a big idea. And if the big idea was not going to be given to Shafarevich, he would have to invent it. Since the late 1970s Shafarevich had been attempting to fill this void, for himself if not for the rest of the intelligentsia. He set about his intellectual search in the methodical manner of the exact scientist, reading everything he could get his hands on. When I visited him in 1995, glassed-in bookshelves lined the walls of his home office – a space so clean, light and, most important, large that it seemed to have been airlifted out of a wealthy Scandinavian country and dropped in Moscow's academic neighborhood. The books were an equal mixture of history and philosophy on the one hand and algebra on the other; many volumes were in French, German and English. In the best intelligentsia traditions, one of Russia's leading nationalist ideologues had a cosmopolitan education.

Shafarevich began with the Leninist assumption that the revolution had succeeded in creating a new type of man. "Since I was a child, I have been taught that our society is something unheard-of, that for the first time in the history of humankind there has grown a society of an entirely distinct nature," Shafarevich offered, apparently by way of explanation for his obsession, so far removed from the world of algebraic geometry. "And in a certain sense, I have concluded, this is true. How we should feel about it – positively or negatively – is a different issue. So I have thought a lot about the nature of this unusual society, by studying the history of Russia and the history of the revolutionary years and the history of socialist teachings, which also interested me: how this ideology was formed."

In the style of a nineteenth-century savant, Shafarevich adopted a truly epic approach to his project. In his first major political work – *Socialism as a Phenomenon in World History*, a book-length opus – he traced and attacked the socialist idea from Plato's Republic through Jean-Paul Sartre. As with his other writings, he overwhelmed the reader with the sheer amount of raw data, plotting a narrative graph through the centuries, then making a sudden, unexplained leap to present his conclusion: in this case, that socialism is an expression of humanity's urge to self-destruct. In its insistence on absolute equality, socialism strips human beings of all that is essentially human, thereby indulging a primal collective death-wish. Shafarevich argues little; rather, like a lab scientist growing hundreds of bite-size socialist philosophies in petri dishes, he strings observations together to support his startling, and ardently presented, theory.

It was his genuine passion that was so alluring to his allies and so frightening to his opponents. Aleksandr Solzhenitsyn virtually deified Shafarevich in his autobiographical book *As the Calf Rammed the Oaktree*. "In our country there are two thousand people who are world-famous," wrote Solzhenitsyn. "But as citizens, they are all zeroes, being cowards, and from this zero level there were only about ten who were able to up and rise, up and grow into a tree – and Shafarevich was among them. . . . Shafarevich is possessed of the most resilient, the fleshiest, the most visceral connection with the Russian land and Russian history. His love for Russia is even jealous – perhaps to compensate for our generation's old omissions? And his is an insistent search for a way to apply his head and his hands to deliver on this love. Among contemporary Soviet intellectuals, I have met almost no one who matches his willingness to die in the motherland and for her rather than find salvation in the West."

Solzhenitsyn's last line sums up the conflict that has divided Russia's intellectuals since the 1840s, when the intelligentsia split into Westernists and Slavophiles. Both trends were nationalist in nature, taking their root in Russia's deeply ingrained inferiority complex in relation to Western Europe. The Westernists, following a tradition begun by Peter the Great, emphasized the European roots of Russian culture and saw the nation's future in a successful transplantation of Western social and cultural achievement. The Slavophiles, on the other hand, brought a heavy amount of mysticism to the assertion that Russia is at root different from the West and therefore better, and that overzealous Westernists posed a direct threat to Russian culture.

When the intelligentsia began once again to emerge as an oppositional social force after the Thaw, the dividing line appeared again. The mainstream of the dissident movement, Solzhenitsyn notwithstanding, appeared to be Westernists. Shafarevich, who was relocating the Slavophile–Westernist divide through his own research, seemed personally wounded by what he perceived as the dissidents' disdain for the motherland.

Referring to those who came to personify the dissident movement, Shafarevich said, "Among them this slogan was always felt: That Carthage must be destroyed, that this is a terrible country that should be demolished to its foundation. I remember times when someone would be leaving [the country], there would be a going-away gathering, and someone would say this toast, 'May they all croak.' And you'd ask, 'Excuse me, who?' Of course, what was meant was that we all should croak. All who remained. Those who remained were slaves, and all decent people left."

There are two questions that have plagued the Russian intelligentsia for a century or more. One, formulated by the writer Nikolai Chernyshevski, asks, "What is to be done?" The other, as posed by the philosopher Aleksandr Herzen, is, "Who is to blame?" Not far below the surface of the Westernist/Slavophile divide lie the two possible answers to the second question: the Russian people themselves – slaves by nature and always longing for a dictatorship – or someone else, such as the West and the Westernists. "The introduction of elements of Western culture into Russia broke the traditional character of Russians, disturbed their national identity," explained Shafarevich. "The West was present in Russia not in the form of foreigners who came here but in the form of the Marxist doctrine, on the basis of which Russia was restructured and which is of purely Western genesis. It has no roots in Russia. It was purely a doctrine imported and forced from without, having been born and having ripened in the West."

The Russian people, then, are victims of the Westernists' hatred of them. In 1981, Shafarevich formulated this view in a book-length essay for which he ultimately became famous yet again and which allied him inextricably with the nationalist far right. The essay, *Rusophobia*, offered a most specific answer to the eternal question of blame. Drawing from his wide-ranging bookshelf, Shafarevich made use of the work of turn-of-the-century French historian Augustin Cochin, who advanced the idea of a "small people" – a minority group that holds views that are in direct opposition to the majority but succeeds in fomenting major social change nonetheless. Cochin applied his theory to the French Revolution, which, he argued, was brought about by a small, driven minority. Cochin's "small people" was a social, not ethnic, concept. Shafarevich, however, gave it a new spin. "It occurred to me that every period of major transformations has its own 'small people,'" he wrote in *Rusophobia*. So who are the "small people" of Russia? "It jumps out at you that there was an especially high concentration of Jewish names among the leaders and executors of actions that were taken at the most painful moments," he concluded.

A morbid joke appeared in Russia in the late 1970s or early 1980s: "The eternal Russian questions are, 'Who is to blame?' and 'What is to be done?' The answer is, 'Kill the kikes to save Russia.'" So they said during the pogroms of the early twentieth century, and so they began to say with renewed vigor in the late 1970s. Shafarevich's essay fell on fertile soil, enriched by the authorities' apparent encouragement of ultranationalist underground organizations such as Pamiat, whose roots date back to that period, and which would mature into the neofascist threat that looms over the country today. Shafarevich, with his outstanding intellectual and dissident credentials, was a godsend to this emerging movement.

Shafarevich's intellectual standing allowed him to play the time-honored game of anti-Semitic thinkers: Spot the Jew. As the world banking conspiracy theory referred to a handful of Jewish bankers in France, so Shafarevich's argument boiled down to identifying Jews among the enemies of the long-suffering Russian people.

In January 1995 an elderly Jewish man approached Shafarevich at the House of the Scholars after the screening of Shafarevich's film *The Third Patriotic War*. "You show Stalinist atrocities and flash the names of the Jews. Why did you do that?" he asked, clasping his own hand nervously. "Oh, the anti-Semitism accusation again," sighed Shafarevich. "That is the way it was."

Responding to *Rusophobia* in 1990, Russian *émigré* writer Valentin Lubarsky wrote in a Russian-Jewish journal published in the United States, "There were 'a lot' of Jews because any number of them is a lot, any number 'jumps out at you.' The rest are merely participants in historical events. . . . Only Jews are not so much participants as the reason for the events." But to support his assertion that that was *the way it was*, Shafarevich cited over a hundred sources for more than fifty pages.

Even for a samizdat publication, especially by an author as prominent as Shafarevich, *Rusophobia* seems to have had an unusually small circulation. The more conspiracy-minded of Shafarevich's former allies later claimed that the mathematician must have withheld his magnum opus from everyone but a chosen few. Perhaps in saying this they simply attempted to underscore that they had not seen the essay until 1989, when, like many other works by many intellectuals that had circulated in samizdat, *Rusophobia* was published in a journal, immediately shocking and alienating Shafarevich's former comrades and throwing him into the open arms of the ultranationalist right, which was coming into its own. The company in which he found himself seemed to make him a bit queasy. In conversation he brushed off most of the militantly nationalist groups as hopelessly marginal. Still, he published in *Zavtra* (Tomorrow), an ultranationalist newspaper, and in 1992 joined the board of the newly formed National Salvation Front, which made heavy use of anti-Semitic smear tactics in its campaign against the government. (The Front shriveled away after the political crisis of October 1993.)

Dabbling in politics for the second time left Shafarevich disappointed again. After the Front all but disintegrated, he left the political stage, apparently to concentrate on refining his voice of intellectual authority. He compiled a three-volume edition of his collected works. The first two black hardcover volumes, containing his philosophical essays, articles and interviews, were presented at the House of the Scholars and, despite a hefty press run of 25,000, disappeared from Moscow's academic bookshops in under two months. (The publication of the third volume, which would contain his mathematical writing, was then delayed indefinitely.)

In 1993 Shafarevich also began work on his film, *The Third Patriotic War*. "The situation in which Russia finds itself now resembles the periods of wars that we call patriotic: the war of 1812 and the last war, the war of the 1940s," Shafarevich explained. "Like in 1812, when Moscow was occupied by Napoleon, as in 1941, when Hitler was already at the Volga – we are in the same situation, in danger of imminent destruction. In both cases, the solution, the victories in those wars occurred because the people realized this very deeply – that the country and the people were in grave danger. Thanks to this, the people were capable of great sacrifice. I think now we are speaking of the same thing: the question is, will the people understand the situation in the same way – as a national catastrophe?"

To bring this truth to the people, Shafarevich used an hour's worth of emotionally charged celluloid, cutting from archival footage of post-Revolutionary famine and Stalinist brutality to himself lecturing in the studio, complete with grandly heart-rending Shostakovich selections and a masterful recitation of Anna Akhmatova's blood-chilling "Requiem." Following the screening of the film at the House of the Scholars, the audience of about 300 sat shell-shocked for a few minutes and then burst into collective praise of the author. "Professor Shafarevich, you are our pride and honor," intoned an elderly female PhD in economics. "Thank you for showing us the light," contributed a mathematics PhD. (It is traditional, at the House of the Scholars, to list one's scholarly credentials before speaking.)

Shafarevich was reticent to discuss the nature of the light he had shown. His job, as he saw it – as the Russian intelligentsia had seen it for over a century – was to wake the People up to the tragic truth. Pushed, he acknowledged that he saw Russia at a divide – between good and evil, between God and godlessness, between its soul and the West. He was not optimistic about the future, but he maintained he had faith in the Russian people.

His surprisingly naive passion, his refreshing – in the post-glasnost age of information overload – belief in the power of words and moving pictures were part of the allure of the film. Another part was the absolution it offered. A crisis of faith was closing in on the intelligentsia. Its liberal-democratic wing, blaming itself for the chaos and bloodshed that followed perestroika, had slipped into passivity; the nationalist wing had grown hysterical at what it saw as a suffocating hold that Western culture had gained in Russia. Shafarevich offered an ingenious theory that allowed him to distance himself from the consequences of a process in which he would have appeared to have actively participated.

In Shafarevich's inventive version of history, both Lenin and Gorbachev are expressions of a single event – the ongoing destruction of Russia. "The Revolution," he explained, "was the preliminary phase of peres-troika. The Revolution destroyed ethnic roots. It destroyed the peasantry. It destroyed the religious world view. It destroyed, to a significant extent, the faith in some united history and national tradition. Once that leveling had taken place, it became possible to take the next step toward disassembling the country's economy, and its science, and turning it into a breeding ground for the West." In other words, the Revolution isolated Russia from the outside and weakened it. Then perestroika exposed Russia to the outside and weakened it. All roads led to the motherland's demise. Naturally, one is compelled to ask who authored such a devilish plan. The answer is "the small people," of course.

He stopped just short of saying that every destructive event in twentieth-century Russian history stemmed from a "small people" plot:

his disciples could fill in that part, allowing him to note, from time to time, that he never said that. He didn't have to: the pressing need was to escape the unbearable weight of responsibility, and in his dance with history he accomplished precisely that.

The service he offered to that part of the intelligentsia that never participated in the dissident movement but idolized, from a distance, those who did, was to free them from the guilt of their old gurus. The old idols, including former Shafarevich allies Sakharov and Solzhenitsyn, had been tarnished by merciless public disappointment. It seemed rather doubtful that the Russian intelligentsia would answer yet another call to vague militancy, even if the next battle was called "The Third Patriotic." But perhaps intuitively banking on the intelligentsia's insatiable longing for meaningful action, Shafarevich, with his uncanny knack for placing himself at the forefront of any trend, seemed to be waiting patiently in the small patch he had cleared of the guilt and hopelessness that plagued his potential allies.

CHAPTER THREE

THE NOUVEAU RELIGIOUS

God lived on Godless Lane.
— Veronica Dolina, a singer-songwriter

Faith, like ideology, deals in symbols. In Russia and the Soviet Union, where a national inferiority complex found its reflection endlessly magnified, these were, for the most part, grand symbols.

Following Russia's 1812 victory over Napoleon, Czar Aleksandr I decreed that a cathedral unlike any other be erected on the hill overlooking Moscow, which lay in ashes after the great fire. In 1827, his younger brother, Czar Nicholas I, fired the planned temple's architect, exiled him to Siberia, and ordered that the mammoth cathedral be erected on the bank of the Moscow River in the center of the city, just downstream from the Kremlin. To clear space for it, he ordered St Alexis Monastery, which occupied the site, razed and its residents moved. Construction continued through the reign of two more czars, to be completed in 1868.

The Cathedral of Christ the Savior was an incomparable monstrosity, a five-onion-headed mass towering over every structure except the Kremlin, with staircase tentacles reaching for hundreds of yards down to the water. It looked like it had always been there and like it would forever remain.

But: "Nothing else shall ever stand firm in this spot," the mother superior of the St Alexis Monastery is said to have prophesied when her domicile was destroyed on the czar's orders. Barely six decades after its completion, in 1931, the Cathedral of Christ the Savior was toppled. To be sure, it took long days. Time after time the construction workers would lay dynamite and light the fuse, causing explosions that knocked out windows and cracked the walls of neighboring buildings – but the cathedral stood. Stalin's orders were final, however, and in the end the ground shook for miles around with the explosion that felled the cathedral.

A plywood fence was erected around the site of destruction. A grand building project was to commence here imminently: the Palace of the Soviets, the ultimate proof of Soviet superiority. In this age, the age of progress, the monument would not be squat and solid like the cathedral; it would extend not only around but upward, adding the gray Moscow sky to the land-and-water domain staked out by its predecessor. It would look like an angular tower on bent granite-and-steel legs, topped with a giant statue of Lenin, an arm extended to point the way. The blueprint was submitted alongside an elevation of the Empire State Building to demonstrate that the Soviet high-rise would scrape more of the sky.

A giant ditch appeared behind the fence. The foundation of the world's tallest building and its first few floors grew out of it. And sprang leaks. The place was a swamp. No high-rise could ever stand there – not even one smaller than the Americans'. Indeed, it was something of a miracle that the Cathedral of Christ the Savior, brief as its age was, had stood so firm.

The Soviet regime never accepted failure, much less admitted it. For two decades the old construction fence hid the shameful hole in the ground with its broken tooth of abandoned construction. The city changed: other high-rises – much smaller – went up; old buildings all over Moscow were razed; war brought panic, violence and destruction; victory brought jubilation and a new wave of terror; through it all, the fence was mended regularly.

In Khrushchev's time the fence came down. Legend ascribes the subsequent stroke of genius to the General Secretary himself: he deemed the leaky ditch destined to be an outdoor pool. In a sense, Khrushchev had no choice. In erecting their monuments, his predecessors had reached up and out; the only direction remaining unexplored was down.

It was called the Moskva Pool, and it was arguably the most remarkable place in Moscow. Long after the Thaw, it continued to symbolize the brief era unfailingly, if unsubtly: the light green rectangle of water, visible from a crowded sidewalk well above it, looked littered with tiny bright dots of swimming caps cutting through a cloud of white steam. It never seemed to lose its romantic appeal: in 1994, after the pool had already been drained of water, artists, writers and poets of at least three different generations gathered inside the tiled ditch to share memories of the pool. Perhaps it helped that the Moskva was a stone's throw from the Pushkin fine arts museum, the Lenin Library and Secondary School Number 57, a notorious hotbed of intellectual rabble-rousing since the late sixties: every Moscow intellectual, it seems, remembers at least once skipping out on school or art class or library research for the sublime experience of swimming in the open air in the center of Moscow on a snowy winter evening.

The post-perestroika mayor of Moscow, the portly Yuri Luzhkov, was active in the *morzh* movement. The word means "walrus," and the people who call themselves that like to swim in winter – not in heated pools but in iced-over lakes and rivers. But that's a red herring, of course – not a symbol. The real reason Luzhkov shut the steaming pool and ordered the resurrection of Christ the Savior had everything to do with feeling grand, czar-like, like the men who had owned this plot of land before him – and a little to do with the reunion of the state bureaucracy with the Church hierarchy.

The relationship between Church and state in Russia was as tortured and as riddled with miserable contradictions as any centuries-long marriage. Rulers had striven to dominate the Church but called on it and propped it up in times of need. It was the rulers of Russia who brought Orthodoxy from Byzantium, so it was destined to become the official religion. One of Peter the Great's reforms lay in legitimizing and structuring the subjugation of Church to state. The czar created a body called the Sacred Synod, which ruled the Church under the direction of a bureaucrat appointed by the czar.

In the tumult of the early twentieth century the Church, like the rest of the country, sought to reshape itself. The clergy's efforts at rejuvenation matched the secular world's struggles step for step. In 1905, at the time of the first Russian revolution, the Orthodox hierarchy resolved to abolish the synod. Twelve years later, just as the Bolsheviks were seizing power, the Church dissolved the synod and recreated the institution of the elected patriarch, abolished by Peter the Great. But the state from which the Church was belatedly divorcing itself was just then being demolished.

The new atheist regime unleashed its war on the Church almost instantly. In the years of the civil war much of the Bolsheviks' aggression targeted churches, which were robbed of their treasures, then had their buildings seized and often demolished. A few years later the government employed its divide-conquer-and-destroy strategy in dealing with the Church. On the one hand, the Church was under pressure to give itself over to the new state, which it did in 1927, when Metropolitan Sergi declared that the Church would forever serve its "secular motherland," the Soviet Union. On the other hand, taking such a stand of cooperation could not and did not protect the Church from persecution. Tens of thousands of Orthodox priests, including the majority of top Church officials, were executed over the years of Stalinist terror.

During World War II the Church was briefly revived by Stalin, who apparently felt he needed help in rousing the troops. After the war the truce between the state and the Church – now headed by Patriarch Sergi, elected in 1944 by eighteen archbishops released from labor camps for this very purpose – continued. According to samizdat sources, the state reopened 22,000 parishes, eight seminaries and two religious academies – though an unknown number of priests remained in camps, to be released by Khrushchev only after Stalin's death. But it was Khrushchev who resumed the persecution of the Church. In 1960–64 he closed more than half of the reopened churches as well as most of the seminaries and monasteries.

By 1975, according to the human rights newspaper the *Chronicles of Current Events*, there were only 7,500 Orthodox parishes in all of the Soviet Union. With the generation of people who came of age in a religious state dying out, with religion consistently denounced by all official institutions, the once-powerful Church was well and firmly marginalized, which meant it also attained a certain romantic allure for the intelligentsia.

To the extent that the relationship between the Church and the state had been treacherous, so the relationship between the intelligentsia and the Church was conflicted. As long as the Church and the state were intertwined, the moral authority the intelligentsia could claim in Russia was precisely the authority the Church lacked. On the other hand, as long as the state subjugated the Church, the intelligentsia was compelled to rally to its defense. The Church inserted an unknown value into the tripartite equation the intelligentsia used to measure its moral health: the state – the intelligentsia – the People. The Church needed to be protected from the state. But if the Church was forced to collaborate with the state, then did allying itself with the Church tarnish the intelligentsia as a collaborator as well?

The first generation of the intelligentsia raged in an argument about its proper relationship to the Church. In 1846 Nikolai Gogol, a great writer facing the end of his creative life, published a book called *Selected Passages from Correspondence with Friends*, in which he sang the praises of state policies on serfdom and, above all, the Church and its clergy. His once-faithful friend, the brilliant literary critic Vissarion Belinsky, entered into an angry polemic with him that culminated in one of the most famous letters in the history of Russian literature, known now simply as Belinsky's letter to Gogol. Berating Gogol for what he saw as his betrayal of the intelligentsia's causes, Belinsky wrote that the Orthodox Church "has always been a pillar of the knout and a servant of despotism," that the clergy "has never been anything but a servant and a slave to secular power," and that "the Russian people hold our clergy in general contempt."

More than six decades later the argument between the faithful and the free-thinking among the intelligentsia continued with the publication of *Vekhi*, or "Milestones," a collection of essays on the role of the intelligentsia in society in light of the intelligentsia's relationship to religion. Some of the leading thinkers of the time accused their fellow intellectuals of taking the country down the godless path to catastrophe. In 1922, when most of the authors of that anthology were, along with dozens of other intellectuals, loaded on the infamous Philosopher Steamer and sent into exile, they believed they had finally been proven right.

So did some of the Thaw intelligentsia, who saw their own and their country's salvation in rejoining the Church. The late fifties and early sixties saw something of a trend among young men from the intelligentsia who chose to become priests. Two of those priests – Aleksandr Men and Gleb Yakunin – would play key roles in shaping the intelligentsia's relationship to religion.

In 1961 the Church adopted a new set of bylaws that made parish priests entirely subservient to local government authorities. In essence, they would now serve at the pleasure of the local soviets; they were also obligated to collect and report information on any children brought in for christening and on couples who requested church weddings; thus not only violating spiritual confidences but exposing believers to potential repressive measures: people could lose their jobs or be expelled from school for attending church. In 1965 two very young priests, Yakunin and Nikolai Eshliman, wrote open letters to Church authorities and the Supreme Soviet asking for the repeal of these rules. The appeal found little support either within or outside the Church, and both priests were fired from their parishes.

Both Yakunin and Eshliman continued to speak out against the Church's collaboration with the regime. Eshliman died a young man. In 1976 Yakunin founded the Christian Committee for the Defense of the Rights of Believers in the USSR. In 1979 he was arrested, tried for the crime of "anti-Soviet propaganda," and sentenced to five years in labor camps, followed by five years of internal exile. By this time he had been a professional resister for nearly twenty years; he had never been allowed to return to being a parish priest, the work he had chosen.

Other priests, some of whom made a conscious choice to resist in ways less visible – and therefore less punishable – continued the parish work among not only the old women who always made up the bulk of any parish but also the young people, most of them educated, who seemed to find their way to church in ever-increasing numbers throughout the seventies. Starting in 1973 a priest named Dmitry Dudko, who served at one of the few functioning churches in Moscow, began a series of sermons on topics suggested by members of the flock, who were asked to pass suggestion notes during services. By the second sermon, the church was filled beyond capacity; Dudko was instantly Moscow's most popular preacher. By all accounts, Dudko was no genius and no poet, and his sermons scarcely more than basic moralizing – he preached the harm of excessive drinking and the virtue of good deeds. Still, in the stagnant atmosphere of the 1970s Muscovites were so starved for public discussion of a topic that really touched them, for any public expression of sincere caring, that they endured long hours in a stuffy, standing-room-only church just to listen to a fairly inarticulate man implore them to be good.

After ten such sermons the authorities put a stop to Dudko's improvisations, moving him to a parish outside of Moscow. His flock, however, followed him there, and he continued his work virtually unhampered for about six years. In 1978 he started publishing a samizdat newspaper, *In the Light of Transformation*, one of a growing number of samizdat and *tamizdat* religious publications. About a year later, soon after the arrest of Gleb Yakunin, Dudko was arrested. He soon recanted, went on television to denounce his "anti-Soviet" activity, and was released to head a prestigious Moscow parish.

By this time the Moscow intelligentsia had another religious beacon. Father Aleksandr Men was a perfect priest for educated religious dilettantes. The descendant of a Jewish intelligentsia family, he was a born popularizer. His many books, published under pseudonyms in *tamizdat*, made religious teachings accessible to people steeped in atheist rhetoric. His small parish outside Moscow became a haven for the tortured souls of the intelligentsia of the Stagnation Period.

By the 1970s a general assumption had taken hold among the intelligentsia: one should support not only the abstract idea of freedom of belief but the very concrete existence and well-being of the Russian Orthodox Church. Its subservient position with regard to the state and the persecution of dissident priests served only to romanticize the Church. Even the presumed KGB affiliations of virtually everyone in the Church hierarchy did not discredit the institution. Nor did the nationalist, imperialist and monarchist beliefs of many of the Church's most fervent unofficial defenders, such as Igor Shafarevich. The desperate passion for a mysterious home of truth and beauty that they so hoped could exist in the Church made members of the young intelligentsia of the seventies accept some very strange bedfellows indeed. In another two decades it would be clear just how strange – and frightening.

During the presidential race of 1996 all major candidates identified as Russian Orthodox believers. All promised the World Russian Church Council that they would make Orthodoxy the official state religion. By this time, thanks to archives opened in 1991 and 1992, the KGB affiliation of several of the most visible members of the Church's nine-member synod had come to light. None of them found it necessary to resign their positions. One of them, Metropolitan Kirill, was the Church's official spokesman.

In 1995 Patriarch Alexi II was given his own quarters inside the Kremlin. The relationship between the Church and the state was in one of its coziest periods. The Russian Orthodox Church was the only major religious denomination not to take a decisive stand against the war in Chechnya. Official Church gatherings became hospitable – and lavish – events for some of the most nationalist and reactionary forces that developed stateside, such as, for example, the recently resurrected Cossack forces, which cheered the war in Chechnya and called for cleansing the country of Jews.

The old rabble-rousers from within the Church were gone. Aleksandr Men was dead, murdered under strange circumstances in September 1991. A clearly innocent man was on trial for the murder. For a time after his death, Men's books were sold on every corner. Now his writing was becoming obscure; at Church gatherings officials used his name as an expletive, along with *universal human values* and *democracy* – words that made them sneer.

Gleb Yakunin returned from exile during perestroika and became one of the leaders of Democratic Russia, the first mass pro-democracy movement. In December 1993 he was elected to the Duma, the lower house of Parliament. Patriarch Alexi II immediately ordered Yakunin defrocked for engaging in political activity and sent a letter to the Duma leadership alerting them to the fact that Yakunin no longer had a right to wear his black priest's robe and large silver cross. Despite flamboyant ultranationalist Vladimir Zhirinovsky's demands for a dress code for Yakunin, the Duma took no action on the patriarch's letter. In 1995, one of the Duma members, the avowed fascist Nikolai Lysenko, decided to take action himself. In front of television cameras, which captured the incident for the entire country – it would be broadcast repeatedly and in super-slow motion – Lysenko grabbed Yakunin inside the Parliament hall, tore off his cross and swung it like a bike chain over the priest's head. The Church offered no reaction.

In 1996 Father Dmitry Dudko once again made a television appearance. Claiming that he had spent seven years in labor camps for fighting the godless Communist regime of the Soviet Union, he called on the audience to vote for the newly Church-allied Communists led by Gennady Zyuganov.

The Cathedral of Christ the Savior was going up at mindboggling speed. The structure that had taken six decades to erect the first time around went up in less than a year in 1995. Christmas and Easter services in the unfinished cathedral drew crowds of invitation-only dignitaries, including all top government officials. At Eastertime red banners went up across Moscow's central streets, just as they had on Revolution Day in years past. Now they said, CHRIST! RESURRECT OUR SOULS!

Perhaps in an effort to resurrect his, Mayor Yuri Luzhkov was presiding over an orgy of real-estate transactions and street renamings that would return to the city, which had once been known for its abundance of golden cupolas, its pre-Revolutionary church flavor. In 1994 he helped the Church reclaim the building that had once housed the church closest to the Kremlin, St Tatiana's Chapel at Moscow State University. For a couple of decades it had been home to the university theater, which now had to vacate. The city intelligentsia recoiled from this inept reach for a moral footing: kicking out a theater that had served as a haven for experimenters and other misfits seemed especially barbaric when done in the name of the Church. The Church, however, ignored mounting media coverage of the St Tatiana's controversy and graciously accepted the real estate.

More than a few people probably kicked themselves then for having given a blanket endorsement, even actively advocated restoring all Church property. A similar wave of belated regret covered the city when the new Cathedral of Christ the Savior started going up. No one had really expected that familiar rhetoric in defense of the Church's property rights would transform reality in a way that literally dominated the capital. No matter where you went in and around the center of Moscow, it seemed, you would suddenly come upon the unfamiliar, frightening hulking mass of the cathedral, which grew by the day.

Still, the St Tatiana's and Christ the Savior controversies were virtually the only sparks of animosity in a time that seemed to lend itself to another flare-up of conflict between the intelligentsia and the Church, something in the spirit of Belinsky. Instead, the intelligentsia was not only maintaining a loyal posture in relation to the Church but experiencing an earnest revival of the feeling of solidarity with the Church that had emerged in the seventies. As the masses flocked to the newly official religion, many in the intelligentsia joined the Church in active ways. They organized renovation works in Moscow churches and spent long days brushing paint off the frescoes. They joined monasteries *en masse*, and some of them were ordained.

Everywhere I went in Moscow, the names of streets had been changed. The first wave of renaming, in 1990 and 1991, struck at some of the most glaring Communist tributes in the city. In the mid-1990s the city was undergoing the disingenuous process of having all pre-Revolutionary street names restored. Often the historical street name contained a church reference, and often the renaming worked to a comical effect. One of the best-known little streets in the outer center of Moscow went from being Godless to Archpriest Lane. In the years just after the Revolution, when it was first renamed, it had surely been an obscure little side street.

Godless Lane continued to be small, of course, but it was now lined with tall apartment buildings and it was famous.

Godless Lane connected a Metro station to a set of apartment buildings populated by writers and actors. It was obviously destined to be immortalized in art and the gossip that surrounds the making of art – and it was. One of the people who lived off this street was Bulat Okudzhava, a poet who put his simple but uncommonly vivid verse to rudimentary tunes and sang, accompanying himself on the guitar, which he barely knew how to play. He started in the early 1960s; several other outstanding poets followed his lead. By the 1970s, there were literally thousands of people who sang their verse to their own simple guitar music; it seemed there was a guitar in every intelligentsia household. The fad gradually transformed into tradition, which was passed on to younger generations. Okudzhava himself, though by the mid-1990s he rarely sang in public, became something of a symbol, not so much of music as of goodness itself. He held meetings with the public in which young people asked him questions and he told them stories from his life and gave them guidance. His status seemed somewhere between a preacher and a deity. A younger singer-songwriter, who was said to be his protégée, sang, "God lived on Godless Lane/And took his poodle for walks."

In that context, it seemed almost profane that Godless Lane was no longer Godless. On a windy November afternoon I drove down Archpriest Lane to see Olesya Nikolayeva, a poet who I knew had a long-standing and profound relationship with the Church. A tall thin woman with long blond hair opened the door. She was wearing black jeans and jumper, which made her look even skinnier; I was surprised in part because in all her printed photographs she had clearly cultivated the well-fed full-bodied healthy Russian woman's look. One adolescent face and then another poked out from behind one of the doors and then disappeared again. Olesya directed me past a sleeping Newfoundland into a large warm room: a bedroom, living room and office in one. I sat down in an armchair, placing my notebook, pen and cigarettes on the coffee table. Olesya looked worried. "I have to warn you right off," she said gravely. "If you are going to smoke here, we have to go out on the balcony. I smoke too, a bit, sometimes, but you see, the frock is hanging right there and we can't have it smelling of smoke, and anyway, sometimes monks come to this room too."

There was a giant black Orthodox priest's frock hanging over the floor-to-ceiling bookshelves behind a large old desk. Here and there behind the glass of the bookshelves stood large black-and-white photographs of monks, displayed the same way many homes displayed portraits of beloved poets or actors. The frock dominated the room, just as its owner dominated my conversation with Olesya, who warned me also that in her answers to my questions she would be guided by her conversations with her husband, the resident priest. She referred to him as Father Vladimir. His name was Vladimir Vigilyansky, and I had known him as Volodia when I was a small child. A friend of the family, Volodia had impressed my childhood mind with his incredible height of about 6 feet 8 inches and his stubborn habit of wearing ripped blue jeans on all occasions. Now for about a year he had been wearing the floor-length black frock of a priest.

In his ripped-jeans days Volodia was a student at the Literary Institute, where he was training to become a critic. He spent a decade and a half working at research institutes, until in 1988 he joined the magazine *Ogoniok*, the flagship of glasnost, to work as a journalist. He became a well-known commentator and earned a reputation among journalists for his inventive mind. He went on to work on the short-lived Russian edition of the *New York Times* and in 1993 headed up the Sunday edition of *Moscow News*, an influential weekly. Whereupon he quit journalism to become a deacon, a forty-year-old man in the role of a religious apprentice, with almost no hope, at his age, of making it to priesthood. Then the fates smiled on him, after a fashion, and he was offered the opportunity to become a priest – at St Tatiana's Chapel.

I had been to the chapel a few days earlier to see him. The building did not look much like a church. It was constructed as a part of the original Moscow University building and had none of the onion domes or porches traditional in Russian Orthodox churches. Instead, it had an elliptical yellow façade with white columns and a cardboard prop of a cross rigged up on the roof. A hand-scrawled sign with the words "Chapel entrance" pointed around the corner to a side door.

Inside, a giant triple-height room with scaffolding apparently holding up the roof was littered with debris. A grand central stairway of the sort one finds in old theater lobbies led, apparently, nowhere; in any case, it was cordoned off with a set of maroon velvet ropes, as out of place in the construction site as the word CHAPEL on the door. The chapel itself, it turned out, was a small makeshift room down a hallway to the side.

I outraged Father Vladimir by asking him about the building controversy. "There has been a chapel here since the eighteenth century!" he exclaimed, creepily shifting into a tone of historical-imperative zeal that made him sound just like the demagogue of the aggressing side in any territorial dispute in this region. "Gogol's memorial service was held here, Anastasiya Tsvetaeva was christened in this chapel. St Tatiana's Day is considered a student holiday because of this chapel. In 1919 the Bolsheviks robbed the chapel, set fire to the icons in the courtyard, and shot the priest. Now we get freedom. What should the intelligentsia do after years of screaming about social injustice? It should immediately give the chapel back. It's no accident that they used to put theaters in chapels — make them into places of entertainment or into stables and toilets."

He picked at his stringy beard and told me with evident satisfaction that the city had banned performances in the building back in 1990 because the structure was deemed unsafe. Renovations, it was calculated, would cost $4.5 million. Finally, the university made a deal with the Church whereby the Church would pay for the repairs in exchange for half the building; a museum devoted to the university's history would claim the other half. It seemed church and real estate were simply indivisible these days. As for the theater, Father Vladimir stressed again, the scandal surrounding its surrender was a sham because it never would have been able to afford renovations of the building.

The Father was worked up. It seemed the property question was a constant thorn in his side. Pursuing a spiritual discussion now seemed out of the question. I asked if I could come again to hear the story of his coming to religion.

A few days later Father Vladimir greeted me with a slightly embarrassed smile. "I didn't end up preparing anything," he confessed. With some relief I suggested we just talk. I figured he knew what I wanted to know. I could, in theory at least, understand how a boy who grew up in Moscow's writing community in the 1960s, weaned on enlightened materialism, would come to find inspiration and answers in religion. What I could not wrap my mind around was how that kind of person, especially one who was an ethnic Jew, could claim a home inside an institution that had for centuries cooperated and collaborated with repressive regimes and was just now undergoing its period of greatest closeness with the state. Moreover, with known KGB agents at the helm of the Church, Volodia was now employed by some of the same people who had persecuted his mother, a writer who was guilty before the state in two ways: she was Jewish and she had published a book abroad. Volodia had been reared in an environment where one would not shake the hand of someone known to cooperate with the KGB, much less go to work for a collaborator.

The priest's story started in the late seventies, when he married Olesya Nikolayeva, who was also the child of a Moscow writer but considered herself a believer, though she did not go to church. Flirting with some sort of belief was fashionable in Moscow at the time; searching young people tended to mix together everything that seemed to push the bounds of Reason. A pseudonymous Christian samizdat author decried the intelligentsia's spiritual dilettantism at the time:

> It always turns out to be a spiritual eclecticism in which Buddhism is intricately intertwined with a left-wing Hegelianism and where Stoicism and the *Naturphilosophie* concept of the neosphere live side by side. Matter is not rejected, but the intellectual does not have a high opinion of it. He also has a low opinion of history and life in general. "Life is a veil of *Maya*," he says along with the ancient Hindu. He also agrees with him that "birth is suffering, old age is suffering, sickness is suffering," and so

forth, right up to the notion that any attachment to the earth is suffering. However, insofar as the Russian intellectual cannot, for some reason, either singly or collectively accept the ways of salvation offered by Buddha – he does not even try to – he continues to live this life, reserving for himself a "spiritual sphere."

Olesya, as she told me, fit that description fairly well at the time. She had been christened but she had barely set foot in a church. She was drawn to Siberian magicians, hypnotists, psychics and all things para-normal. And she figured she should have the kids christened. Volodia did not object, so the couple took their two elder children in hand and set off for a church outside of Moscow. This too was a well-traveled path. At the time, the regulations requiring priests to report christenings and church weddings were in force, and being caught participating in religious ritual could lead to significant professional problems. Communing with God in an out-of-the-way rural church was, if nothing else, a more appropriately private experience. One could generally learn from acquaintances which parishes were safe.

"The priest asked me if I had been christened," Father Vladimir recounted. "I responded that I wasn't because I didn't consider myself a believer, so it would be dishonest. He responded that there was not a single person in the world who could state with absolute confidence that he was a believer. He reminded me of the line from the New Testament: 'Help me in my disbelief' and told me to use it in my prayer." Volodia had probably never encountered that sort of acceptance. The Soviet intellectual was shaped by sets of conflicting absolutes – absolute officialdom and its absolute and categorical denial by the "differently minded." Perhaps one of the main characteristics of the Brezhnev era was that it left no room for doubt. Volodia, by all accounts, had always been racked with doubt. In one of her poems, his wife described him this way:

> "Life is a tricky thing," he sighs,
> staring off in the darkness.
> Or "It's time to relax," decides,
> giving a sigh of relief.

> Either making far-reaching plans
> > or aimlessly playing with matches,
> He is either unshaven or ill,
> > or panicked, or covered with sweat.

What a relief it must have been to stumble upon a place that could serve as home to that sort of convulsive doubt, to have dispensation to ask for certainty and admit its absence.

Volodia returned to that out-of-the-way church eight months later and asked to be christened. "I was expecting you," the priest told him. I asked what he had gone through in the intervening time. Father Vladimir seemed to grope for words. "Let's say I had – I had some innermost revelations." I waited, hoping he would feel he had left something unsaid. "You know, Berdiayev wrote to Shestov," he said, citing two early twentieth-century Russian philosophers who turned to religious issues later in life, "that the Christian religion is entirely based on personal experience. So it is useless to try to explain. I had revelations of an innermost nature."

I was hoping Olesya would articulate more of the nature of this all-important transition. She was, after all, a poet, a woman, a lay person, so I thought she might be better with words and less reticent about using them. She got to the subject of revelations right away by telling me she had her first mystical experience at the age of eight, when a girlfriend set a midnight rendezvous with her in the garden. "She had called me to tell me a secret: that she wrote poetry. And I just had this feeling that there had been a horrible mistake, because it was I who was meant to write poetry. It was as if an elder had prophesied this." The same thing, she said, happened when she was fifteen and saw a young man from across the hall at the Writers' Union clinic. She heard a voice say, "This man shall be your husband." Years later she set out in search of the man (not all that difficult a task in the close-knit writers' community), who would later become Father Vladimir.

As she told me the stories, Olesya maintained the pointedly detached expression of a person who is revealing some difficult truths about herself. To me it sounded like the sort of things acquaintances may share over an idle lunch, attempting to cut the boredom with surprising recollections.

Olesya tried to clarify. "I have always known that God exists. When I was four, I had this thought that I should devote my life to Him. And the thought scared me: 'But I won't be strong enough! I won't be able to give my *all*!'"

As a young woman, she went through the usual Moscow intellectual's chaotic selection of retyped writings by Shestov and Berdiayev, of treatises on Buddhism and random excerpts from the New Testament. She had friends who had already made their way to the Church, who used to make pilgrimages to an elder who somehow became known as a prophet for the intelligentsia. Elders, in the Russian Orthodox tradition, are elderly monks who often live as recluses, away from a monastery, and serve as spiritual advisers to their own flock of sorts. An elder named Seraphim Tiapochkin was a legend among a certain part of the Moscow intelligentsia, but, Olesya said, her friends who visited him guarded their relationship jealously and never took her along.

Then a mystical coincidence transpired. Olesya went on a reading gig of the sort Moscow writers often signed up for to make some money – a trip to a provincial town where she would have to read her poetry. On the way back, she accidentally boarded the wrong bus, which stopped right in front of a rural church. As it turned out, it was Good Friday. She summoned her husband, who came and spent a week with her in an entirely alien environment. "We landed among monks, and we have stayed in that milieu since. Monks would stay in our apartment when they were in town."

She lit up as she told me that over the following two or three years she and Volodia got their Christian education from young monks who would come to their apartment for heady discussions. She was in her late twenties then, he in his early thirties. They used their education and verbal skills to grill the monks, questioning them on the meaning of politics and the meaning of life, on the moral status of religion in the Soviet Union – this was, Olesya pointed out, at a time when Father Gleb Yakunin was in prison. Their monk friends would come over dragging their theology textbooks and engage them in a friendly battle of words.

"We became marginal figures of sorts," Olesya recounted. "On the one hand we had writer friends, and on the other hand, the monks. They would sometimes meet one another in our home. And then later they would fall in love with one another."

How magical it must have been, in the stagnant atmosphere of the early 1980s, to have a secret existence, to have broken out of any number of closed little worlds that made up Soviet life then. Each of them – the dissident circle, the "differently minded" circles, the writers' circle and the mathematicians' circle, not to mention the truly privileged circles – was wrapped up in its own tin curtain, behind which even the bravest of ideas began to go stale after a time. Inside each of those circles, people lived in the suffocating safety of like-mindedness, while here, in this dusty apartment off Godless Lane, a battle of ideas raged from day to day. Olesya described their interaction with a regular at the house, a young priest whom "we were always trying to knock out of his saddle. And if he didn't know the answer to something, he would write the question down and would take it to his spiritual adviser. And sometimes he would really open things up for us with his explanations." Olesya and Volodia started doing some work for the Patriarchate, condensing religious tracts they were given into shorter texts. Whole new areas of thought opened up to them. Schooled in the Soviet system, they could not have imagined an entirely different system of knowledge. "I had read textbooks on psychiatry, and that was child's play compared to theology. They would bring us entire volumes on the passion of anger, the passion of vanity. It was all incredibly interesting."

And surely incredibly refreshing to probe tensions that occupied few other people – and to feel a higher calling. The new knowledge and sense of purpose breathed new meaning into all of life. She told me a story that, were it not for Olesya's important confidential tone, would have sounded like girlish gossip to me. "My girlfriend's husband left her," she began. "She is beautiful and well-known, plus she is fifteen years younger than her husband. She thought of herself as his muse and valued her own skepticism very highly." She gave a cryptic description of the husband from which I could surmise that he was a very famous and very well-loved man who lived nearby. "Once she came over here drunk, a mess. Then she decided to pray to God to give him back to her. We started going from elder to elder, and as we went around, these were such wondrous adventures for her. The husband came back because we had turned all the monasteries upside down. We spent several days with one elder, and during that time the husband had all four tires slashed on his car, so he couldn't go see his mistress. Another time he hit his head and couldn't go; another time he got a blister on his foot and somehow got this idea that he should put vinegar on it and burnt the skin and couldn't leave the house. So in the end he stayed.

"Through all this she came to the Church," Olesya concluded in a tone of genuine satisfaction. "All this ended when God reached His goal, because He knew that such a proud woman couldn't be reached in any other way."

The sense of higher purpose seemed to change everything: it justified spending so much time with a despondent friend, pulling dozens of other people into a very personal conflict, and, finally, telling the story to me. What some people wouldn't give for that sort of security in one's own position.

Just that, in fact, was what her husband had come to lack a few years earlier, when he hit upon that condition of middle age, compounded by the end of perestroika, that made everything seem utterly pointless. "I was at a loss," he told me of the moment when he decided to give his life to the Church. "I had grown utterly disappointed with journalism and publishing. I suddenly felt like an old man. All my colleagues were about ten years younger than I, and I wouldn't understand them, and they listened to me with empty eyes. For example, they would say, 'We should publish a list of the children of billionaires around the world.' What for? 'It's interesting.' But I didn't find it interesting at all. Or I would say, 'Let's have famous people do interviews with people no one knows, like taxi drivers.' And they would say, 'What for? That's not interesting, they don't know how to do that.' And it was like that with everything.

"And the other thing that really drove me crazy was that journalism did not have a higher goal. There were some immediate goals that we achieved. But no overall concept. They don't have any idea what the point of their lives on this earth is. One of them said to me, 'The meaning of life is life.'" Father Vladimir looked at me for signs of understanding and I attempted to portray surprise – for lack of outrage, for I also thought that the meaning of life was life itself. He concluded sadly: "I feel more affinity for a person with any convictions at all, even ones that are the opposite of mine."

That was key. Intent on his search for true believers, he had really risen above the substance of their beliefs. He had moved beyond everything that was ripping Moscow and the rest of the country apart: the politics, the war, the elections. The day we spoke, he was going to attend a meeting of the Writers' Union together with another writer cum priest, one who adhered to far-right nationalist convictions and had nearly come to blows with Father Vladimir in their lay days. Now, Father Vladimir told me, they could only laugh at their petty passions. "All barriers fall before eternity," he told me. "All parties divide people, and not along the lines along which they ought to be divided."

I wondered how far his detachment extended. It was late 1995. Outside the doors of the decrepit chapel, most people believed that the fate of the country was being decided: the next resident of the red building complex across the street would be chosen in a few months, and, some people believed, catastrophe would soon follow. How would he vote?

"A priest cannot have affinities," he explained. "If I could vote against, I would. But I cannot vote for. You gain a different outlook on history, you see. We cannot wish persecution upon the Church, of course, but periods of oppression always brought out a lot of saints. It's a frightening sort of dialectic. I cannot wish fascist or Communist rule upon this state, but who knows – it may be the way of the seed that dies so that thirty or sixty others may sprout. It is better not to interfere in all that. And whatever regime there is – whether it is Communist, fascist, democratic or Liberal-Democratic, we shall pray for it. For any regime."

A blessed state. He was entirely free of the nauseating feeling of helplessness that was sweeping in waves over Moscow. This was a quality Father Vladimir shared with the many other people I had interviewed about finding God after perestroika. There was the mathematician forced by glasnost to look up from his calculations; he lost his equilibrium and his vision of the future, and regained both only after he became a priest.

There was an elderly research chemist who lost his funding and his sense of usefulness but felt human again after he threw himself into the study of religion and started preparing white papers on introducing moral frameworks into modern Russian society. There was the lesbian writer who had spent her entire adult life in the cozy quarters of marginal underground and was terrified by the flood of fresh air and daylight – until she devoted herself to work on restoring a chapel, which once again enclosed her life within clear boundaries. All of them had reached out from under the rubble of everything they had known, grabbed something they thought might be God, and felt the incomparable relief of connection with others and, perhaps, a future in spite of any struggle that might rage around them.

The question I had so wanted Father Vladimir to answer, then, lay in a reality he had left behind. The reasons he chose to devote himself to religion were of the same paradoxical set that any educated middle-aged man or woman anywhere in the world might cite for abandoning the familiar frameworks of rational godlessness. The desperate need for meaning and commonality did not simply overpower the intelligentsia's concepts of honor and moral action – it rendered them irrelevant. For much of the differently minded intelligentsia any argument about the unacceptability of collaboration and the consequent need to maintain a distance from the Church held meaning only so long as it yielded a righteous sense of community. As perestroika and middle age blurred the secular boundaries of right and wrong, Volodia, like many others, had to move to a sphere in which shared certainties and ideals were still guaranteed.

CHAPTER FOUR

THE MYSTICS

If there is one thing that the Soviet regime managed to burn into virtually every brain, it is that a good theory, a really good idea can explain the world. The whole world with no exceptions save for those that prove the rule. Few consciously rejected the official big idea, and even fewer went so far as to deny the need for and desirability of one; the rest were left to find a big idea of their own, their own certainty to protect them from danger, death and fear.

Some were able to locate a private code that helped them explain the world to themselves; others needed to assert their discoveries publicly. Konstantin Kedrov, for example, credited himself with discovering something he called "inside-out," and he very much wanted the world to know about it, since he was quite confident his discovery was nothing less than revolutionary.

Konstantin Kedrov was a small man with skinny legs, a large belly, a straw-colored beard and features that, while unremarkable, fit together so awkwardly they made him look like an aged Pinocchio. Being a poet, he was everywhere poetry was to be read. He was a one-man cultural factory, always announcing one initiative or another. He published one issue of a poetry newspaper; he gathered poets into groups; he arranged for the publication of group collections. He worked very hard to make himself indispensable, and his reward was the association of his name and his words with the work of people in every way more remarkable.

To others, he may have seemed pathetic. He always felt his calling was poetry, but his poetry was rather limited. His timing was perpetually off. The first thing he ever said to me, without a hint of irony or even self-consciousness, was: "I had the misfortune to be born a poet in this country. But I was unlucky – Andrei here – " he nodded at Andrei Voznesenski, one of the best-known poets of the Soviet era, "entered poetry, and then the door shut behind him. He was being persecuted, and I was then only a student, so things were much harder for me." It was hard for Kedrov even to get himself persecuted properly. In the early nineties, when anyone who would be considered liberal tried to boast a history of repression, Kedrov complained that he was fired from his cushy teaching job at the Literary Institute – but in 1988, at the height of perestroika. Whether or not the incident indeed had anything to do with the KGB, Kedrov was doomed never to have the heroic biography of the long-suffering poet, that classically Russian narrative for which he longed his whole life.

Still, I honestly don't think Kedrov ever felt the hanger-on he appeared to be. He believed himself to be in possession of a greater truth. Within five minutes of meeting me, he declared, "In my lifetime I have made two discoveries." The first was what he called the metacode, "the single code for all things animated and inanimate." The second was the "inside-out" effect. "Imagine," he instructed me, "that the space outside you is actually your inner space. That is, everything around you is your insides, your kidneys and gall bladder. This is how Neil Armstrong felt when he set foot on the moon – he said that the universe became a part of him. For people to understand this would equal giving up the idea that Earth is flat."

Isaiah Berlin described the Russia of the 1840s as a place where any idea fortunate enough to penetrate the border from the West was assured an exhaustive hearing. "You must conceive," he wrote, "of an astonishingly impressionable society with an unheard of capacity for absorbing ideas – ideas which might waft across, in the most casual fashion, because someone brought back a book or a collection of pamphlets from Paris (or because some audacious bookseller had smuggled them in); because someone attended the lectures of a neo-Hegelian in Berlin, or had made friends with Schelling, or had met an English missionary with strange ideas. . . . When such doctrines were promulgated in the west, they sometimes excited their audience, and occasionally led to the formation of parties or sects, but they were not regarded by the majority of those whom they reached as the final truth; and even those who thought them crucially important did not immediately begin to put them into practice with every means at their disposal. The Russians were liable to do just this; to argue to themselves that if the premises were true and the reasoning correct, true conclusions followed; and further, that if these conclusions dictated certain actions as being necessary and beneficial, then if one was honest and serious one had a plain duty to realise them as swiftly and as fully as possible."

A hundred and fifty years later, the sorts of ideas that appealed to Russians were different – the preference for socio-political thought over mystical and religious belief was reversed – but the unfathomable willingness of entire layers of the population to embrace a new idea and practice it with total devotion remained the same. Berlin had attributed this phenomenon in part to the small size and isolation of the intellectual circles, which simply lacked the critical mass to foment new ideas. This condition, too, remained similar. True, research institutes had proliferated during the Soviet period, but external restrictions and internal inertia kept them from becoming environments for the free exchange of ideas. So Russian thinkers continued to gather ideas where they could find them, try them on for size and then often cultivate a missionary passion for spreading the new truth.

In the later years of the Gorbachev period, such proselytizers were able to attract enormous crowds for mass hypnotism sessions or public revelations of a religious nature, as when a former Komsomol (Communist Youth League) leader who had renamed herself Maria Devi Christos declared herself the Messiah and predicted the imminent end of the world. By the mid-1990s the supernatural, paranormal and mystical had been assimilated into the mainstream. Before the December 1995 parliamentary elections, the Duma press service organized a press conference for a psychic who predicted the winners and losers, along the way dispensing advice on personal body care. The leading liberal daily, *Izvestia*, the country's most firmly establishment newspaper, had hired Konstantin Kedrov as a columnist whose topics ranged from literature to the sciences with a mystical bent. In early 1996, when a group of physicists in Switzerland succeeded in producing an "antimatter" particle, he wrote a triumphant piece, announcing that the point at which time turns back and space turns into its own opposite had finally been discovered. He was convinced this was scientific proof of his "inside-out" effect.

Kedrov believed that he had lived through two transcendental moments in his life, when he was fortunate enough to experience the "inside-out" effect. "At that moment," he explained to me, "time suddenly turns in the opposite direction, starting to pass from the future to the past instead of from the past to the future, and this way it encompasses all of time at once." To buttress his point, he showed me an illustration in his book *The Poetic Cosmos*, which he published in 1989 and defended as a doctoral dissertation at the Institute of Philosophy – for decades the country's main arbiter of thought – in 1996. He assured me that a diagram that looked like a large X showed "the way Einstein has time turning inside out at a speed higher than the speed of light."

Kedrov had devoted much of his life to trying to describe this phenomenon, which, as he never tired of saying, was capable of changing people's thinking about everything forever. He referred me to a poem of his entitled "The Computer of Love," a long series of two-line verses in all capital letters, which, he explained, was often misinterpreted as some sort of romanticism or cynicism or some such thing – when in fact it contained a "key" insight into the "inside-out" effect:

> THE PERSON IS THE SKY INSIDE-OUT,
> THE SKY IS THE PERSON INSIDE-OUT.

Kedrov had gained this insight during a peak experience in 1958, when he was fifteen, and reaffirmed it during a similarly blessed moment in the seventies. "This moment is accompanied by the sensation of weight-lessness," he told me. "The body may be raised off the ground, and it acquires a kind of glow. And the most amazing thing is, you have the feeling of sensing everything, and you lose the measure of space. You experience your death as though it were in the past. The past, future and present seem to exist simultaneously. And you experience great disappointment because after a few hours these sensations dissipate, and you can reproduce them only as a model."

Kedrov had studied as much of the body of Russian poetry and prose as he could in the fruitless search for an adequate model. Even those who considered his ideas harebrained acknowledged that he was extraordinarily well versed in nineteenth- and twentieth-century Russian literature. Kedrov concluded that many writers and poets had experienced and attempted to describe the "inside-out" effect but that no one had done it justice. He suspected, too, that some writers had knowledge of the phenomenon but held it in secret. Considering the earth-shattering significance of the discovery, a certain conspiratorial discretion was quite understandable.

Kedrov himself attempted to engage in a sort of one-person conspiracy, disguising his metaphysical quest as literary research. His search for "inside-out" in the body of Russian and foreign literature bore unexpected fruit. Leafing through his weighty *Cosmos*, Kedrov pointed out its numerous tables. Like other chronically misunderstood people who finally manage to get a journalist's ear, Kedrov said over and over, "This is very interesting," or, "This is especially interesting," or, "Here is another monumental discovery of mine."

Kedrov's discoveries are too numerous to list here, so I will limit my narrative to the most outstanding. There was, for example, the discovery that any address book or telephone directory in any language in the world lists twenty-eight letter categories, regardless of the number of letters in that particular alphabet – and this happens to correspond to the twenty-eight phases of the moon. Kedrov also found that world literature consisted of several distinct categories of characters. There were the sun characters, who were characterized by their integrated nature and included Don Quixote and Dr Faust. Then there were the moon characters, who tended to be split like the two halves of the moon – e.g. Tristan and Isolde, Romeo and Juliet – or like the different phases of the moon – including for some reason, *Crime and Punishment*'s Raskolnikov and Jaroslav Hašek's good soldier Schvejk. There were also North Star characters. Kedrov called this phenomenon "the metacode." He also created a table that explained the "star code" of literature, which linked literary characters to different constellations. This, incidentally, extended well beyond literature, explaining, among other things, the appeal of the McDonald's double arches: they resemble Cassiopeia.

"And here is another extremely interesting thing, simply amazing," said Kedrov. "As there exists the Mendeleyev Table [of chemical elements], equally objectively there is a table of the approach to the black hole." Kedrov explained this seminal theory, but it would be difficult to relate it here: after all, what Kedrov was showing me was an entire doctoral dissertation.

One of the people whom Kedrov always dragged around with him, or, perhaps, whose coat-tails he hoped to ride – one could never quite tell with Kedrov's literary-promotional activity – was Vadim Rabinovich, a chemist, an inventor, a poet and a philosopher. An odd thing about Rabinovich was that he was accomplished at all those things. He had patented dozens of inventions, published several books of poetry and a couple on cultural history, and he held doctorates in chemistry and philosophy. The field of study for which he was best known was alchemy; Rabinovich had written two books on alchemy, and one of these was itself styled as an alchemist's treatise, with each chapter containing a recipe and seven interpretations of it.

Kedrov recommended that I speak to Rabinovich about "the mysterious" – a popular euphemism for everything paraknowable. I went to see him at the Institute of Philosophy, a large yellow building across the street from the Cathedral of Christ the Savior; when he was giving me directions, Rabinovich stubbornly instructed me to go across from the Moskva Pool.

Rabinovich, who was sixty, seemed like the sort of man who had made peace with the hopeless inferiority of those around him. He had no interest in interacting with strangers. He was polite: he took part in group readings whenever he was invited; he gave interviews. But once he read the poems he had prepared he would often doze off, dropping his large round head onto his huge belly while his colleagues read their work. When I came to interview him, he wasted no time listening to my questions, launching immediately into a prepared monologue. He quickly explained that as long as he could remember, he had been fascinated by those who combined the incompatible, as he himself had done with chemistry, poetry and philosophy. Hence the interest in alchemy: "they thought it elementary to combine three ounces of sulphur with two ounces of anger – what interests me is chemical magical thinking."

When Rabinovich was done explaining his concept of humanities scholarship – an engaging, if fairly pat, introduction to culture studies – I asked what he thought of Kedrov's work. After all, Kedrov defended his dissertation at the Institute of Philosophy and Rabinovich had served on his committee. Rabinovich seemed uneasy for a moment. "Well, I gave him a positive review, because he is my friend," he said honestly. "But in substance I was very critical. He is searching for a formula to explain all of culture. Here he cancels out cultural uniqueness. When the accent is on invariability, history disappears. That's absolutely counter to my approach."

All right, but what about the phases of the moon over different literary characters, time turning back and people ingesting the universe? Was this kind of exploration perhaps helping rejuvenate the Institute of Philosophy and the institution of Russian philosophy, demonstrating that the limits of reason can be renegotiated? Rabinovich's small purplish lips gathered in a slightly displeased purse. "In this age of mental timelessness, we have drifted away from the rational tradition. From Aristotle and Plato through Marx and Heidegger, we have lost trust in Reason. But mysticism should not be juxtaposed with Reason, because Reason contains within itself room for flight of spirit."

I had set out to learn how the gap between Kedrov's sort of eclectic mysticism and Rabinovich's kind of earthy rationalism had been bridged. I had thought Rabinovich would be able to explain to me how it came to be possible for someone like Kedrov to find a place within Russian academe; he had succeeded only in convincing me that it had been an incredible feat. Still, Kedrov was not unique. The newspapers were full of stories about biologists who had built an immortality chamber at one of Moscow's research institutes, linguists who had located the hidden astral references in all of the world's languages, Moscow City Council deputies who were drafting a new school program that would incorporate the basics of magic and astrology, and so on *ad infinitum*. There had to be a link, an intermediate stage between the traditional scholarly and other establishments and their inventive new members.

I suppose as I returned home from my interview with Rabinovich, I was, shall we say, sending out slightly desperate vibes that would have attracted the missing link – were that sort of thing possible. As I entered my apartment, the telephone rang. A soft male voice introduced itself as Vitaly Tatko, the director of the Institute of Consciousness. He was calling about an article I had recently published in a Moscow magazine: he wanted information on contacting someone I had profiled. After answering his questions, I started grilling him about his institute, the name of which intrigued me. It was a private research group, he explained, that worked in a number of different areas: psychoanalysis, Creutzfeld-Jakob disease.

"You see," I said carefully, "I am interested in the mysterious."

"Well, I don't really know you, and I do not know your views," he responded. "Which is why I could not mention it right away – you have to be careful, you know, because you never know what sort of reaction you may encounter. But that has been one of our main areas of study since the beginning."

Tatko came over a couple of days later. He came armed with clippings – exactly the sorts of newspaper articles that testified to the acceptance of mystical pursuits within academic institutions. Speaking in a lilting high voice, punctuating his speech with careful but frequent gestures, Tatko told me of his work on paranormal phenomena. Ten years earlier Tatko, a psychophysiologist, was approached by an acquaintance, a successful experimental physicist who had started measuring everything that could be measured about healers, hypnotists and others who laid claim to extraordinary psychic ability. The physicist, Eduard Godik, had collected a great amount of data but had no one to interpret it. "His predicament resembled that of an X-ray technician who has made marvelous shots but knows nothing about the nature of the object," Tatko recalled. "I was invited as an interpreter."

This was 1986. For a couple of years Godik and his staff had been recording the brain waves and the heat emissions of such people as the famous Dzhuna, said to have kept Leonid Brezhnev going for the last years of his life, and who could now gather crowds of hundreds of thousands. "The thing is," said Tatko, "I didn't see anything in that data. I told them what I did see, but that was trivial. And there was nothing else."

But Tatko had been invited to advance theories. And truth be told, he had always harbored a fascination not so much with paranormal phenomena as with everything that veered off the narrow path of Soviet scholarship in his field. The study of psychophysiology had been one of the most tightly controlled areas of academe. The shadow of the great Ivan Pavlov, the discoverer of conditioned reflexes, loomed over every scientist who would venture between the mind and the brain. No allowance was to be made for humans being human and possibly different from Pavlovian dogs, or even from one another. "When I attempted to define the topic of my doctoral dissertation in the area of consciousness," Tatko remembered, "I was told over and over that consciousness was none of my business, that it is a public phenomenon and not to be studied on the level of the individual."

So Tatko was primed to grab any project that lent itself to studying the individual as a separate entity. "If we are talking about *psycho*-logy, about the soul, then how dare we attempt to average these souls out?" he was exclaiming in my kitchen ten years after he turned decisively away from this approach. "Lion Feuchtwanger wrote that it is certainly possible to derive the portrait of the average contemporary, but the face on the portrait will belong to no one, so it will be a lie. Furthermore, the result opposes the foundation: the individual."

Here was a project that took as one of its basic premises the unique abilities of various individuals. For Tatko, it probably mattered little whether or not the individuals possessed the abilities to which they laid claim; the temptation lay in the opportunity to study persons as distinct from one another. Tatko spent every day of the following three years on the project.

Of course, the basic flaw of the study was the utter absence of proof that something was there to be studied. The problem, as Tatko concluded, was the methodology that traditionally governs experiments. "You see, Godik had these incredibly sensitive methods, which registered much more than we knew, but he could not register anything that gave any reason to connect it with paranormal activity, and he never did. But since I was invited as a theoretician, I tried to think beyond this. So, theoretical thinking calls for some boundaries. I thought, maybe they cannot register anything, in principle. And I provided a theoretical basis for this approach.

"It's very simple. The thing is, all physical equipment that we use and most of the theories we can apply are constructed in such a way that we need serial observation. We need to be able to replicate them. It's a sort of mechanical-piano approach: we assume that if you hit a key, it makes a sound, and if you don't, it doesn't." Tatko supposed that the secret of paranormal activity, if it existed, would lie in its exceptional nature. That is, each time it would require a unique set of circumstances, including the extraordinary mobilization of the subject's abilities and an unusual sensitivity on the part of the object. From his copious files he extracted notes on some foreign scholar's paper that had once drawn his attention. The scholar had conducted experiments with cats and shown that when an animal was in mortal danger it could throw all its abilities toward preventing it – for example, using not only its motor faculties but its visual and auditory cortex to avoid falling into a vat of hydrochloric acid. Tatko latched onto the suggestion that exigency could override evolution. "Nobel Prizes were given out for the discovery of the visual cortex – they found all sorts of specific tasks there," explained Tatko. "And I suppose that's all there, but that is not the point; the point is that in addition there is also the possibility of doing something completely different. Extrapolating from the cat to the individual, I could say that sometimes we differ from ourselves more than from our neighbors."

In other words, Tatko theorized, there were times, albeit not very frequent, when what we believe to be impossible became possible. There were people, albeit not very numerous, who could, perhaps only in those times, do the impossible. In proffering this theory in a time in Soviet history when the impossible seemed to be happening, Tatko did the impossible by breaking out of the boundaries set for all of Russian academe.

"This was a wave of liberation," he said. "Liberation is always a good thing in scholarship, like when you have thought that something is a certain way and then suddenly it turns out to be completely different. Or when you have observed different things in the world and then suddenly they merge and turn out to be one thing. This sort of change in thinking is the most important part of scholarship. And we were liberated as individuals, from this incredible repression that meant that when things were interesting to people for no reason other than that was what we got up with that morning – these things stopped being the object of manipulation of that giant mechanism that was obsessed and terrified that we were going to understand something about something that we clearly did not need and that they did not need and that could have caused complications, which they did not need.

"It so happened at the time, fortunately, that the Academy of Sciences had no money, which was a glorious circumstance, because it became clear that the pressure the Academy had exerted had rested not on scholarly knowledge, as we had all thought, but on the ability to publish, reproduce and the rest. When the money disappeared, the Academy powerful gradually shriveled up. And then I no longer had to be doing one thing at my research job, using utterly reductionist methodology, while thinking that in reality the world was far more complicated. The opportunity to get away from that sort of double-think was probably the main reason I was interested in this area of study."

When I heard about Yevgeny Anisov, I thought he and Tatko were potential allies. Anisov was a fifty-nine-year-old biologist whose stated goal in life was to rally scholars to raze the walls of academe from within, to take on objects of study that had been declared out of bounds. He was retired from his research institute and identified now as more of an activist than a scholar. At one point he had tried to organize rebellious scientists into a group he called Biopolitics, but this attempt had foundered. As he explained to me on the telephone, he had devoted his life to helping other scientists' daring studies into print. He said he would bring some of the studies to our meeting, and I would recognize him by the booklets he would be carrying.

We met at Moscow's Lenin Library on one of the hottest days in the history of the city. The soles of my shoes were sticking to the melting pavement as I approached the building. Several people seemed to be waiting for someone at the entrance. One man was wearing filthy blue pinstripe trousers, a gray pinstripe suit jacket buttoned over a shirt that might once have been white, and a brown wool beret that fit oddly on top of a head of unruly yellow-gray hair. He was holding a transparent plastic bag filled with small books, which he thrust at me as soon as I approached him.

"You'll read these and understand everything. These are fundamental. I have reliable information that this kind of work is going on both here and in America, but in both countries it is classified as top secret. These are about emanations from eyes. Aleksandr Blok has this poem about how he can stop women with his eyes, but not all of them – it depends on their level of sensitivity. I can tell just by looking at you that you are sensitive to that sort of thing.

"You see, I started thinking about this when I was twenty." Anisov's vocal chords sounded damaged, perhaps by decades of smoking. His voice was so weak he always seemed like he was straining to scream. "I started thinking about why some people had talents, like Mozart or Tchaikovsky or Babel, and then I realized that evolution was to blame. Prehistoric man was absolutely talented in all areas, from the artistic to the sexual. Then, through evolution, he began to acquire specialized ability. Those who are talented today are people who retain something of the prehistoric man. Some people know this, but it is kept secret because the issue is too sensitive. But I am hoping that the global mental crisis that awaits us in the year 2000 will move them to declassify this information.

"Because you see, it explains everything. Absolutely everything."

CHAPTER FIVE

A WESTERN TRUTH IN
A RUSSIAN HOME

People in war zones talk about the oddest things. Some obsess about their personal lives, keeping each other up nights desperately tugging at faraway tales. Others find a scapegoat to rag on at any opportunity. On a bright January morning in 1995, about four weeks into the war in Chechnya, I was riding in an armored minivan, which had once belonged to a cash collector, through the filthy little town of Nazran, the Ingush capital, where most journalists and human rights activists were based. In the back seat, the stars of the Russian human rights movement, all former dissidents, were working themselves into a state of manic joy mocking their scapegoat of choice: feminists.

Sergei Kovaliov, who at the time appeared nothing less than the rightful successor to Sakharov – *ergo* a living saint – reveled in recounting an anecdote about members of the first known feminist organization in Russia, Maria, coming to show their samizdat magazine to a friend of his for comment. "Instead of giving them the comments they expected, he did a textual analysis of their entire magazine," Kovaliov recounted, chuckling. "So they came back to find out what he'd thought of it, and he said, 'The word *phallus* is used more often than any other – twenty-two times – and the word *patriarchy* – '" The usually refined men in the back – two professional human rights activists, a diplomat and a member of Parliament – expressed their thorough approval in pubescent guffaws.

The members of that first feminist group had shared the fate of many dissidents: blackmailed with threats against their children, they were forced to emigrate. One would have thought this would entitle them to solidarity on the part of these men. The *modus operandi* of the dissident movement, to the extent that there was a movement, was in protesting all attempts by the state to persecute people for practicing their ideas. Kovaliov and others who worked on the *Chronicles of Current Events*, the newspaper of human rights violations, spoke up in support of Orthodox religious, Slavophile and nationalist activists, virtually all of whom, after perestroika, ended up on the other side of the barricades, fighting their one-time defenders. The incompatibilities had been clear two decades earlier, but back then the disenchanted and the persecuted knew their only slim chance of survival lay in having a common enemy.

The Caucasus is an incredible region. There are hundreds of different peoples and tribes, most with their own language, customs and patch of land, and that patch of land itself usually houses a mind-boggling variety of ethnic groups, each with its own language and customs. The people of the Caucasus are infinitely proud of this diversity and the tolerance it proves, and they like to boast to visitors about it. The Ossetians will point out the Jewish quarter and tell of heroic young men who ran into burning synagogues during the war; the residents of Dagestan will boast that fifty languages are spoken in their tiny region. But each Caucasian people has a group – just one of the neighbors, usually – whom it loathes. The Ossetians love everyone, but if they see an Ingush, they'll kill him. Or so they say. The Ingush drive eight hours from Mineralniye Vody to Nazran instead of taking the two-hour direct route through North Ossetia. Never mind that the two peoples, like all of the Caucasus, suffered many of the same disasters and attacks for centuries; they will never recognize their commonness. There are fifty languages spoken on the tiny territory of Dagestan, but – and so on, *ad infinitum*.

Driving through the Ingush city, I realized the human rights dissidents weren't unlike a Caucasian tribe in this way. They had performed miracles of tolerance, at times making tolerance itself a goal that justified much. But they too needed someone they could snub, refuse to take seriously, ridicule – in short, some one group to which they could do all the things that their country did to them. Perhaps women's groups offended their romantic idea of themselves as successors to the Decembrists, the czar's officers who staged a single picturesque protest on a bright December morning and suffered for it in exile – where their wives had, of course, followed them (it stands to reason that the two best-known women dissidents, both remarkably courageous thinkers and organizers – Larisa Bogoraz and Yelena Bonner – continue to be known first as the widows of great men, Anatoly Marchenko and Andrei Sakharov). Or perhaps the introduction of what they dismissively referred to as "sexual characteristics" into their world of disembodied words and ideas made them feel too vulnerable, reminding them of their own physical selves, which could so easily be destroyed. Whatever the reason, feminism played the role of Ingush to the dissidents' Ossetians: the one group that was to be neither supported nor even tolerated, but always and rudely dismissed.

All the better for feminism, really. Because few people bothered to think about it until the late 1980s, few people stood to be disappointed. Unlike other great trends in Western social thought – Marxism, say, or the concept of human rights – it was not burdened with decades of hopes, dreams and lives devoted to it by the people who saw in it Russia's salvation. Indeed, when feminism finally wound its way to Russia, appearing mostly in its American incarnation, imported by Western students and tourists who seemed to flood the capital cities at the end of perestroika, the apparent reason a not-insignificant number of women embraced it was that they saw it as the key not to their country's but to their own personal salvation. Each of them had to contend not only with the intelligentsia's crisis of faith but with her own slice of the disasters that befell Soviet women with the introduction of the market system, when women's unemployment soared, women's representation in government fell, and the few rights and benefits women had been guaranteed by the Soviet system got swept away by a combined force of rampant capitalism and a new traditionalism.

In the spring of 1993 I was working at a new weekly newspaper, where an endless stream of Moscow intellectuals came marching through making their pitches or setting their conditions to editors. When a woman in her late thirties with disheveled red hair, brimming with a voluptuous sort of self-confidence, marched in for the first time and made herself comfortable, I knew she belonged to the category of writers who set their own terms; at least she seemed to think so. She declared loudly and repeatedly that she would write for the paper only if she could edit a "feminist page." She explained patiently to anyone who happened to be in the room that she was not merely a writer but a feminist writer.

As I learned later, Masha Arbatova was a playwright of dubious talent but an incomparable socialite. She belonged to the breed of writers – those who came of age in the 1970s and who would have been at their most productive in the 1980s – who entertained little hope of getting published or produced and whose identities as writers fed less on writing and being read than on belonging to a certain writerly community. In these intelligentsia subcircles, circumscribed by favorite quotations that served as passwords – instant evidence of literary preferences and expertise – writers created for one another, and one another's company and comments sustained and nurtured them. Words were a private instrument, and words borrowed and repeated, as well as words spoken in response to the written words of others, were equally valuable, equally needed. In the late 1980s words suddenly broke the circumference of these groups, along the way asserting their individual worth, and the distinct worth of those who had written them down. Many of the writers of what became known as the "mute" or "silent" generation started getting published and becoming known; many others didn't. Masha, whose plays focused obsessively on human reproduction – abortions, out-of-wedlock children and gynecology were her trademarks – found that she encountered the same "censorious clichés," as she put it, on the newly liberated theater market. Her plays continued to be rejected as too risqué; one director suggested she change either her protagonist's profession, which was gynecologist, or the topic of that play, which was abortion. Her cozy writerly circle opened up and let Masha and her words out, but no one else seemed to appreciate them. Like so many of her contemporaries, she was suddenly spiritually homeless.

Masha Arbatova, being Masha Arbatova, found the explanation of her troubles at a party. "At some writerly get-together I met a couple of foreign women," she recounted to me at the café at the Central House of

Arts Workers, which, as she informed me as soon as I got there, was the only place in town left for creative people to hang out. "These women really helped me relax, because like that Molière character who did not know that he spoke in prose, I did not know that what I was facing was discrimination against women." Years of being offered a session on the producer's couch in exchange for a staged play or a higher fee suddenly made sense, as did what she realized was a "patriarchal marriage," which was just then starting to crack under the pressure of societal change.

For about fifteen years Arbatova had been married to a man whom she described as a "state singer" — the performer of approved songs in an approved style for approved audiences, which vanished as soon as the music scene was allowed to shape itself. "Like all men of that generation, my husband was completely broken when he had to start everything over. I was the opposite: I started supporting the family, paying for the expensive private school the children attended. I started getting involved in all sorts of projects, writing articles for which I was paid in hard currency. So I put the issue to him: 'I make the money, so you've got to do the work around the house.' He was rebelling: he would do things either half-way or poorly, or he would nag me by saying I'd made a sissy out of him."

The "foreign women" at that party embodied what Arbatova wanted to be. "I had a child's reaction to them," Arbatova told me. "I wanted to be like my friends. I saw how free they were, and I wanted that. And, of course, when you go through the right door, you start attracting things — books and such." Out went the husband; in came the glamorous life of a "feminist writer."

Arbatova founded a women's club, which she called Harmony. Advertised as a group for raising women's self-esteem and liberating their potential, it quickly evolved into a sort of weekly kaffee klatsch and exercising circle. In 1994 Masha became a regular guest on a new television talk show called *Doing It Myself*, where she played the role of the feminist commentator. She offered her brand of earthy commonsensical feminism for every situation presented on the show. In a discussion of whether it is proper for a man to keep house while his wife works, for example, she would say it was the right arrangement for the times and for the couple, while her "traditionalist" opponent would warn against its dangers.

With the talk show regularly making it onto the list of the ten most-watched television programs, by the mid-1990s Arbatova was the country's best-known feminist. She coquettishly complained to me, "The show really interferes with my image." She bemoaned phone calls from strange women wanting to "sign up" for feminism, having to pretend to be her own look-alike when accosted on the Metro, and being thought of as a "professional feminist" rather than a playwright. She did not, however, try to disguise the fact that our interview was wedged in an all-day leisurely meeting with a cellular-phone-equipped friend, a television producer, with whom she was working up a pilot for a new women's television program.

Fame certainly had its uses – and not just because when a play of Arbatova's was finally staged at a small Moscow theater in 1995, it drew the critics' attention because everyone had heard of the author (it got mixed reviews). For one thing, Arbatova's social circle was forced to, as she put it, "forgive" her – take her back. "You see, the intelligentsia sees feminism as something that the West funds – because no one could possibly call herself that voluntarily." She was shifting from socialite gabbing into a mercilessly insightful attack; one could get the impression it was indeed the television that destroyed her image by making her thoughts seem glib and overly simplistic. "The intelligentsia has always seen human rights as something that protects them but not as something that could protect *from* them. This is very important, because while they fought for heaven on earth, they sowed incredible evil all around." She was referring to the sort of attitude I encountered among the human rights activists in Chechnya. But, she said, "for a while they pointed their fingers at me, saying I was a lesbian or a man-hater, and then they forgave me."

That was a relief, clearly. She would hate to be thought radical. Not so much because that would be impolitic or because it did not reflect her politics but because her feminism was never about politics. It was strictly a feel-better proposition. The result of her feminist enlightenment about which she most liked to brag was her new husband, a "male feminist," as she called him, who did not mind housework. Arbatova believed it was

DEAD AGAIN

just fine for a man to keep house. Other than that, she didn't exactly challenge the patriarchy – she'd hardly heard of it.

If Masha Arbatova was the face of Russian feminism, then it was a face that belied the mind, if not necessarily the heart of the creature it represented. Feminism first took hold and flourished among academics and intellectuals – mostly sociologists and psychologists fascinated with Western psychoanalysis and its use in feminist theory. Their trajectory tended to be the opposite of Arbatova's, whose great feminist insight was followed by a successful reduction of the new idea to its logical bare minimum; for them, as for most people who fall in love with something they know nothing about, the initial discovery led to unexpected intellectual complexities and uncomfortable mental adjustments.

Anna Tiomkina fell for feminism in the early 1990s, when she was a guest researcher in sociology at a New York university. "In America I saw feminists for the first time and started to understand what this is about," she told me, blinking self-consciously behind bottle-thick glasses – a caricature of the intellectual. Her longtime fascination with psychoanalysis, an interest in critical theory of any sort, and years of experience as a sociologist studying social-change movements all came together in one glorious circle around feminism. Perceiving what she called a "non-static theory with unlimited opportunity for me personally to participate," Tiomkina decided to write a book about Western feminist theory for Russian scholars.

There were just a few obstacles. For one thing, in Russia, where her research institute had stopped paying out salaries, Tiomkina would never be able to write the book; she would have to continue getting fellowships or guest-lectureships in the West. By the time I met her at a feminist conference in a St Petersburg suburb in the summer of 1995, she had been living away from Russia for about three years – first in the States, then as a guest instructor in Finland. For another, once Tiomkina started writing what she had envisioned as a traditional sociological text, she found that the distance between her and her subject was so great that what she wrote was simply boring. "All this stuff had been interesting for me to read," she explained, "but there was a barrier – where there was I and there was a certain object of my study. And it was feminist theory that taught me that there can be a different relationship between the subject and her object of study, that I can take part. So the project transformed into one where I was writing the theory and my own version as a more-or-less typical representative of Russian reality, though also somewhat integrated into the European situation. As a result I started paying more and more attention to the issue of what in feminist theory is relevant and what is not for Russia."

So she took the giant, barely conceivable leap out of the spectator scholarship on which she and other Soviet intellectuals were weaned and into the heady process of active idea-making. And collided with another obstacle, arguably the hardest for a writer to surmount. Language. Virtually all feminist theory exists in words that are either historically wrong, ideologically repulsive, or simply unknowable for post-Communist Russia. Take *patriarchy*, for example. "It sounds painful to me," Tiomkina cringed. "I use it anyway, but it's not exactly applicable. For example, it looks like in America there was really a patriarchal society, to use the terminology, and a woman who belonged to the middle class – she was bourgeois, she did not work, she was completely dependent on the man, she was limited to the family – that was what the fifties and sixties were like. We didn't have that situation in Russia or, say, in Scandinavia, where the woman always worked, where the bourgeoisie in its purest form was limited, they always had a woman who participated in labor, which led to a different feminist approach, where little is said about patriarchy, about oppression, but more about a gender system or a gender contract."

Not that *gender* is any better. The word, which has no equivalent in Russian, was dragged into the language by a couple of groups of feminist researchers in Moscow and St Petersburg in the early 1990s. They formed their "gender research centers" and used the word in their writing, which, combined with dozens of other imported words, made their work difficult to understand and their circle hard to penetrate. Tiomkina decided for herself that *gender* was acceptable since she was writing for other academics. "All right, let *gender* be. But then there are horrible things like *womanhood* and *sisterhood*, which I don't know what to do with at all, because there is no way I can translate *womanhood* into Russian. And then there are those terms that I don't like, like *oppression* and *suppression*, which I use with footnotes explaining in what contexts they are used."

There is no word in Russian that might describe, as *womanhood* does, the female condition, but, of course, *oppression* and *suppression* do have Russian equivalents — it's just that these are words that, being key Marxist terms, produce a violent allergic reaction in post-Communist Russians. And it is these words, perhaps more than anything else, that make feminism repellent for people who resisted Communist ideology. But at least they are familiar. Which is more than you can say for terms that come from psychoanalytic theory, banned in the Soviet Union and popular but only superficially known in contemporary Russia. The only terms, of those employed by feminist theorists, friendly to a Russian ear are liberal terms — the language of rights and equality, which sounds good but bears little relationship to Russian reality. The result, Tiomkina summed up with a sigh, is that "since there is no language or the language is parallel to us, we don't see it."

There was something to this wholesale hopelessness that fit the more heart-rending traditions of the Russian intelligentsia. Kovaliov and company, eat your heart out: this woman was on a mission that had its impossibility built in at the most basic level — the level of language. For in the overly verbal culture of the Russian intelligentsia everyone knew that thoughts cannot stretch beyond words. So, I asked Tiomkina, inasmuch as language determines mentality, aren't you trapped in a vicious circle? I waited for an answer filled with the noble pathos of a visionary. I knew she would say that a feminist world view breaks that limitation, that shaping the language would ultimately shape society. She shrugged her freckled shoulders, which stuck out awkwardly from under a sun dress: "Listen, if a person doesn't want to read a book, she puts it down. That's not my problem."

My mistake: she was on an academic's mission to illuminate, not on the intelligentsia's mission to enlighten.

*

Anyway, the market on enlightening the masses was already cornered. There was a woman whom friends called "the grandmother of Russian feminism." A St Petersburg newspaper printed an interview with her under the headline SHE CAME TO GIVE US LIBERTY. Olga Lipovskaya had the biography of an educator if ever there was one. A girl from the provinces, self-taught and self-made, goes on to found a home-made journal that blossoms into a research center and makes her an internationally recognized authority. A classic.

She rendered the story less extraordinary. "My life span fits into the historical process perfectly. Until 1980 I was a housewife and I was a secretary in the district government's executive committee, which was a job that enabled me to put my son in a good school. And when I started to produce the journal, it was already almost legal and I was satisfied with the readership of ten people that it had. After I put out the first issue in 1988, I went to journalists' clubs, and then I joined the Democratic Union, where I got my political training. At the same time I worked as a fixer and a translator, then I started to travel abroad and meet people, and I got article assignments, which built my reputation, and then I got a very lucky chance with a German women's funding agency." Granted, you could write a contemporary-history textbook using Olga Lipovskaya, born 1954, as a study guide. But you have to be Olga Lipovskaya to surf historic opportunities like that.

Olga and her two sisters were raised by their grandmother in a small southern Russia town. She was in love with languages – Italian especially – and planned to study them in the big city of Leningrad. At Leningrad State University hundreds of young people trained by expensive private tutors competed for the few seats that were not already spoken for by people with connections; a provincial girl did not even figure in the contest. She tried and failed a couple of times before becoming a hippie, hitchhiking around the country, often getting picked up by police. After a few years she drifted back in from the margins just enough to wind her way back to St Petersburg, marry, then marry again and then again, have a son and later a daughter, work as a ticket seller, a secretary, a nightguard.

Like much of her generation, she temporarily suspended her ambition but not her passion. She picked up languages where she could – a course here, an acquaintance there. In the five years that we had been friends I had seen her communicate in English, French, German and, I think, Polish. Her English was good enough for simultaneous translation. She said it wasn't exactly self-taught: she learned it from a couple of Canadian boyfriends she had in the seventies. In the early eighties she read all the English she could find. In 1983 or 1984 she came across a book called *Sweet Freedom*, a history of British feminism, and "discovered a slew of ideas that I shared." Some of these ideas had crystallized in 1980, during a long hospital stay following an accident. "I had quite a lot of time to think and write – these funny notes entitled 'The Complex of the Soviet Male,' in which I described a man who was on the one hand dependent and on the other hand tyrannical." Jean Baker Miller's *Toward a New Psychology of Women*, read in 1985, was a "peak experience." Friends started to give Olga other books having to do with feminism, and in 1987, at the dawn of perestroika, a friend who published a samizdat journal of translations asked her to contribute something. She did a couple of chapters from Baker Miller.

At the time a quasi-underground group in St Petersburg, calling itself Club 81 in honor of the year of its formation, performed the functions of a publishing elite for the samizdat world. The club included editors of samizdat publications who would gather periodically to promote and critique their production. The reaction to Olga's first samizdat contribution was, as she recalled, something like, "The subject matter – ugh – but the translation's not bad." She added, "If this was their reaction, for me it served as encouragement."

In 1988 she inaugurated her own journal, *Zhenskoye chteniye*, which means "women's reading." It was eighty pages of typewritten text – translations of Western feminist articles and some Russian women's writing (including a Masha Arbatova short story, about abortion). The first four issues had a carbon-copy run of ten, with seven legible, and that, Olga maintained, was enough. Issues five and six were reproduced on a photocopier. The use of copying equipment had been legalized, signaling the end of an era of hiding – and of underground publishing. Issue six of *Zhenskoye chteniye* was its last.

At the time Olga was working as a night-guard. She's done a good job of summarizing the rest. In 1993 she received funding for a research and education center in St Petersburg. Five years earlier she had recklessly been printing her telephone number and address in her journal; now she had a small circle of acquaintances who shared her interests and views. Some of them became staff members of the St Petersburg Center for Gender Issues.

They underwrote a couple of studies. They held a few conferences. They spent most of their time arguing and fighting about which one of them should be doing what when, and in what manner. Olga rolled with the times, which were cruel to people who got their ideas about the way things work from books. After a couple of years her project had sacrificed a good half of its staff, and she forfeited the wholeness of her vision of the world. "I consider myself nowhere," she told me. "I do not like people with Soviet mentality, and I do not like people with Western capitalist mentality – although my career would be considered successful by their standards.

"I want to go back to those times when I was working as a night-guard and I spent every fourth night there and I would take my portable typewriter with me and after all the mechanics left I would sit and think. And on salary day I would get drunk with them, and I liked earning their respect. And I slept in a guard booth with mice everywhere and there was a dog named Amour, which means love in French, and I didn't know how all these ideas would be implemented – I just liked my life."

I had to make corrections for the the vodka we had downed in the course of this interview on a no-longer-white night of late summer 1995. Vodka tends to bring responses closer to what the interviewer wants to hear – or vice versa. Or perhaps it just tends to dress thoughts in colors of wistful nostalgia. Stripped down, I think, it was simply what she told me at another time: "I thought I would implement my dreams, but my dreams are very much in the field of theory, of information. In two and a half years I have found there needs to be a lot of practical work. I feel much better when I can give women jobs as translators, or when I can teach ten girls to work on a computer. This is much better than giving a lecture, because they are not interested – they are not interested *yet*."

Lena Mashkova has dedicated herself to making them interested. It takes some manipulation – or, perhaps, just cunning. She began her two-year course in gender studies at a small private college in Naberezhniye Chelny, a large industrial town in Tatarstan, the land of the Kamaz truck factories, with a semester devoted to the results of studies she had carried out as a cub researcher at Kamaz in 1988.

The way she had come across her subject was, on a personal level, an accident and on a federal level, a policy. It was the year after she got her graduate degrees in sociology and psychology – she had first been a mechanical engineer, but after a couple of years at Kamaz found that she would spend the rest of her professional life making the same few drawings while her husband, with whom she had finished college, and other male colleagues moved up. She came back to Kamaz with a "feminine" profession and was immediately given a responsible assignment: that year Kamaz was to be the site of a conference on international labor law, and Lena was to prepare the event, complete with a study on the status of women at this industrial giant.

The numbers she got were simple and striking. Women at Kamaz earned 74 percent of what men earned; only 3 percent of women, compared with 29 percent of men, received advanced training at the plant; of 70,000 women, 41,000 worked in illegal, harmful or dangerous conditions. Lena crunched her numbers and dutifully sent them off to all the industrial bigwigs and party bosses who were supposed to review her paper before it was presented; it seems they were all so certain they'd get their Potemkin village of women's equality that they did not even check the text.

A few minutes after twenty-seven-year-old Lena presented her paper, one of the country's most prominent women academics, a sociologist who had flown in for the conference, patted her on the shoulder and said, "Consider your dissertation done." The next morning, a black Volga picked her up at 6.30. "So they take me to this place where all the bosses are, and each has a copy of my paper. They tell me, 'You used faulty methodology' and that I have to resign in twenty-four hours." Then they delivered her back to the conference, where she committed her next transgression: instead of keeping a good façade, she told some participants what had happened. They in turn told someone else, a high-placed woman apparatchik who could pull strings on behalf of a hapless young sociologist. It so happened she had an ax to grind with the Kamaz administration, which had allowed the disastrous *faux pas* of having her picked up at the airport by a conference bus instead of a private limousine. The next day, Lena got another Volga ride to the same place. "The same people who'd been ready to slaughter me the day before were now saying, 'Such good methodology.'" She not only did not have to resign but would head a committee on improving the status of women at Kamaz.

The committee remained just a concept, but over the next few years Lena defended her dissertation under the famous woman's tutelage, stubbornly using Kamaz as her research site, spent a semester in New York taking a gender studies course and coming to think of herself as a feminist, returned to Kamaz staff and left again, finally becoming a one-woman feminist production in good old Naberezhniye Chelny. She started an organization called Femina, which conducted sociological studies, provided gender-awareness education and produced a television program.

For a while, my attempts to figure out who actually *was* Femina, this fountain of feminism in Tatarstan, encountered a wall, not necessarily intentional but nonetheless impenetrable. It seemed it was Lena doing it all and passing herself off as an organization. I could almost believe that: six feet tall, apparently present at every feminist conference or parliamentary hearing of consequence, she seemed to need no sleep and be able to down unlimited amounts of alcohol without showing any strain. As I figured out eventually, though, the mysterious Femina was Lena and her girls – the ones she had been teaching to be feminists.

Feminism is not considered a nice word in Naberezhniye Chelny. During the second semester of the course she began teaching at a small college in 1994, one of Lena's students came to class in tears. Her father had sent a recently published book, one of the first feminist collections in Russian, down the garbage chute. He had apparently told her, "You should be getting married, not reading books with words like that on the cover." The book was called *Feminism in Prose, Memoirs and Letters.*

That was the second semester. During the first, Lena claimed, she did not even mention the frightful f-word. She just showered her students with numbers, which she had accumulated over her years of studying at Kamaz. She'd dreamed of this moment since 1987, when she first saw women's lives on graph paper. She imagined that some day she would make a movie, in which a monotonous voice-over would recite the laundry list of the putative rights of Soviet women while the screen rolled Lena's numbers. "For me, those figures sing," she remembered. "I would walk around with that voice-over in my head, and I would see illustrations everywhere. This was the time of the worst food lines, and I would go into those empty stores with desolate counters, and in the middle of the store there would be a wire cart with green tomatoes – and the long line. And the voice would play in my head."

Now that the figures were far more dramatic – Kamaz had ground to a halt, first firing virtually all its female workers – Lena was making regular half-hour programs for local television, produced by a small team sponsored by a US foundation. That's in addition to the twelve sociological studies under the auspices of Femina – basically, her girls' term projects, which ranged from oral histories to analyses of newspaper clippings. And the gender studies course, which she had taught not only at the college but also over the Internet to ten groups of women in different cities.

That last one brought a bit of a shock. The groups were all different: unemployed women in northern Perm, academic researchers in Moscow, and teachers in Novosibirsk. The last group had a truly collective approach to everything, including essay tests. In their final one they wrote that they had liked the course and: "We have conferred as a group and we agree fully and utterly that a woman's natural purpose is to be a wife and that the husband should be the one earning money and bringing it into the home and the wife should be grateful to spend it."

"At first I thought that I had done something wrong," Lena confessed,

"but then I realized that I was getting simply a cross-section of views."
In any case, her objectives were fairly modest: to give women some
exposure; to make girls think about redistributing the chores in future
families; and, most important, to teach girls how to use computers and
read a bit of English, making it easier for them to get jobs in the future.
Once you've seen those numbers, you become a very practical sort of
feminist.

"Imagine you are wiping a big pot with your behind! Now wipe it clean!
Get it all out!" About thirty women aged between eighteen and sixty,
dressed in sweat suits and business suits and frilly dresses, moved their
bodies in a way that looked so pleasurable it seemed wrong to watch it.
This was applied feminism too. This was Masha Arbatova's Harmony
club.

The shop-talky but no doubt worthy goals of "raising self-esteem" and
"reducing stress levels" were, as it turned out, achieved through an
evening of group exercise, group tea drinking, group makeup appraisal,
culminating in a group flamenco dance. The evening started out with
the women in a circle, all of them looking like they had rushed to the
Central House of Arts Workers from their business meetings, lectures,
errands and baby duties – something, anyway. They performed a series
of moans and groans and imaginative muscle stretches. They broke for a
Mary Kay saleswoman, who promised not only to sell them expensive
makeup but also to teach them to use it, which is music to a Russian
woman's ear. Then actual music started and the women formed rows at
the other end of the room, and their heels and skirts clicked and flared in
the unmistakable rhythm of flamenco. By this point, it was eleven o'clock
at night. They probably had husbands, children, mothers and work
waiting for them at home, but they would rather be here on Monday
nights. This too was very practical feminism, even if its rituals may have
appeared bizarre.

Of course, bizarre is in the eye of the beholder. If I thought that
weekly groaning sessions were a strange thing to offer women as a
solution to their problems, most people in Russia at any time found the

very concept of an intellectual approach to tangible painful problems a very odd thing indeed. More even than the telegenic Masha Arbatova, what people like Anna Tiomkina, Olga Lipovskaya and Lena Mashkova made their life's work was a rare and difficult thing to fathom. A reporter presented with a list of Lena Mashkova's activities asked incredulously, "And do you expect that this will somehow benefit women?"

"I do not want to play savior to anyone," she responded. "I am simply arranging my own life, creating my own space, filled with people with whom I can discuss these things. Life flows like a river, where I am a whirlpool, and some woodchips get sucked in, and that makes community."

As for the big unresolvable question of what such a foreign and abstract set of ideas as feminism can really do for long-suffering but passive Russian women, Mashkova dismissed it as the nonissue it was. "I realize that it offers no solutions," she said. "For me, the level of ideas is far removed from the level of reality. Some people say that Communism was a good idea but nothing came of it. For me feminism is the idea of partnership, of equal rights, and it does not lose its charm just because it does not become reality. The only thing I fear is to be forbidden to do this work."

One would have thought the dissidents and samizdatchiks and other assorted intelligentsia would have recognized themselves in this willingness to live for an idea profoundly unlikely to penetrate reality. They probably would have, if they had not been afraid to look. But they were and they didn't.

All the better for feminism, really.

PART THREE

THE SEARCH FOR A PLACE

CHAPTER SIX

THE BUSINESSMEN

The scene outside a Moscow outfit called Manhattan Express on a cozy September night would be easily deciphered by any New York or London clubber. The fidgeting in the sizeable crowd, the perceptible push toward the velvet ropes from behind which several young women scrutinized the crowd, the burly security guards looking on – this was a happening night spot. The crowd was aggressively self-righteous. Tatiana Lavrionova, the executive producer at Moscow's hottest movie studio, was helping with face control, and she looked overwhelmed. "These must be all techies," she stated dejectedly. "Movie people are never so stylish!"

This bunch was stylish. It looked airlifted from a Calvin Klein ad shoot and dropped in the center of Moscow. These were a subset of the "New Russians," a term popularized in 1994 to denote a mythologized new breed that managed to ride the wave of economic and social change. Most Russians felt badly battered by the changes. More than half the population now lived below the poverty line. The number of suicides had increased by 40 percent in just two years. "New Russians" were the aberration: people who had money, style and a belief that life was good and getting better.

Deriding New Russians quickly became a national pastime. They were too rich, too proud, too aggressive. In intelligentsia circles it became *de rigueur* to note that they had little culture and no taste, what with their gaudy nightclubs and audacious clothes. But a careful reading of the newspapers and a survey of one's acquaintances would invariably point to the fact that Lavrionova was right: overwhelmingly, New Russians were techies. That is, they were the intelligentsia's children; indeed, just a couple of years earlier they had been the intelligentsia. These were computer scientists and physicists, mathematicians and engineers – the people who graduated from the country's prestigious high-pressure technical colleges and went on to work at universities and defense ministry research institutes, along the way shaping the intelligentsia's culture. Quirks of the system conspired to create this unlikely social class: for one thing, unlike people involved in intellectual pursuits in the humanities, techies were generally left alone by the overseers of ideology. In addition, since over 80 percent of the techies were employed by the defense industry, many of them spent their lives in closed towns populated entirely by their colleagues (there were twenty-two such towns just outside of Moscow and forty more throughout the country). One of the paradoxical results of such segregation was that the techies, ensconced in a rarefied, intellectually rigorous environment, produced a steady stream of trends and fashions that would dominate the intelligentsia's thinking and behavior.

In the idealistic 1960s they made up the nucleus of the dissident movement, which resisted the regime; the movement was launched by the mathematician Aleksandr Yesenin-Volpin, inaugurated with a protest that involved ninety-nine engineers and mathematicians, and drew much of its inspiration from the physicist Andrei Sakharov. In the repressive 1970s, when much of the intelligentsia sought refuge in nonpolitical activities, the techies made two of them into full-fledged fads: mountain climbing and folk singing. The first Moscow concert of Vladimir Vysotsky, the folk-singing popular hero of the 1970s, took place in the Culture Hall at the Kurchatov Institute of Theoretical Physics, the birthplace of the Russian atomic bomb. In 1981, the same hall hosted Moscow's first rock concert.

Another decade later, techies led the way in conquering the newest frontier: business. The man reputed in 1994 to be the country's richest, massive-scam artist Sergei Mavrodi, was a computer scientist cum stock market shark; the country's second-largest bank, Tver Inkombank, was founded by physicists; the man who controlled some of the country's largest investment firms, as well as its main television channel, Boris Berezovsky, continued in his spare time to curate his research lab at a mathematics institute; small and medium-size businesses seemed downright dominated by the techies. Sometimes I had the feeling that any newly and conspicuously successful person would certainly turn out to be a techie. The composer for an immensely popular singer, for example, was a physicist; his former colleague at the Kurchatov Institute was a leading alternative-fashion designer – the one whose show at Manhattan Express was so popular.

"We studied to be engineers or physicists, and now some are composers and others are traders," declared the fashion designer, thirty-three-year-old Nikolai Polushkin. "This should not come as a surprise: techies – especially Kurchatov physicists – have always been the most progressive people in Moscow, and now we are starting our own thing and creating a new culture." Polushkin's assertions were as self-serving as they sounded: he graduated in 1985 from the Moscow Engineering and Physics Institute, known as MIFI, an elite institution with a pipeline to the Kurchatov Institute, where Polushkin worked until 1988. He started sewing in 1986 – when, following the Chernobyl nuclear power plant disaster, he realized that nuclear physics would never again be the cushy field it once was. At Manhattan Express that night he was showing the conceptual creations in silk that had recently landed the designer on the front page of *Izvestia*. He claimed his success in fashion – his outfits retailed for over $1,000 – had come naturally, in no small part because he had moved up in the world together with his peers. "Gradually, I became better," he said, "and I kept making clothes for my friends, who were becoming store owners, presidents of computer companies, producers."

"All of our techie friends have gone into the music business or the clothing business." I was beginning to feel like I was collecting advertising copy for technical education. Now I was speaking with Larisa Protasova, a 1986 MIFI graduate in computer science who, with 1986 MIFI systems-engineering graduate Liudmila Abramova, had been designing and manufacturing women's clothing for two and a half years. They were among Polushkin's peers who struck out into business. "It became very difficult to survive in the hi-tech field," explained Abramova.

"MIFI professors now make 200,000 roubles [then about $65] a month."
(In the old days, they made a couple of hundred dollars a month and
could afford virtually anything in the state-controlled economy; now that
prices had reached Western levels, they were poverty-stricken.) "So these
people, though they liked what they were doing in the sciences, turned
to their hobbies, and those became businesses."

Abramova and Protasova made an odd-looking couple: the first was
barely over five feet tall, bodacious with a copper helmet of hair; her
dark-haired partner was extraordinarily tall and lanky. No wonder that
the two engineers who had never been able to find suits that fit properly
decided to make elegant clothes "for real women, not models," as they
proclaimed in unison. They borrowed about $1,000 from Protasova's
husband and bought a sewing machine and some cloth. Now their $100
suits and $20 blouses were carried by seven Moscow stores and ordered
by about thirty regular clients. After just four months in business, they
were able not only to quit their engineering jobs but to start hiring
seamstresses. At one point they had ten people working for them; now
they had cut down to the four best workers – all former engineers.
"We've given up categorically on professional tailors," chirped Abramova.
Techies, she said, "make the best workers: they are the most responsible
and the most inventive.

"Techies are practical-minded. We know that if you are given
information, there must be a solution. It may not be the solution you
envisioned, but there is always a solution." Protasova nodded enthusiastically. Here the pair was no longer speaking about clothing manufacturing: this was their rendition of the philosophy that had enabled techies
to stake out their sort of sovereignty in Soviet society. Their quest for a
feeling of liberation and a sense of personal control had taken them to
snowy mountaintops – an ingenious solution to the suffocating predicament of the Soviet intellectual. Now they were applying their mental
skills to surviving under chaotic conditions. Like other techies-turned-
entrepreneurs, Abramova and Protasova claimed that what distinguished
their colleagues from the rest was an ability to react quickly and
constructively.

Speed – lightning speed – was key. One who wanted to hold on to a semblance of social status and economic well-being had to race the poverty figures, the suicide statistics, the skyrocketing vodka consumption. Those few who succeeded in reinventing themselves "simply had no other choice," argued Mark Nemoiter, who in the late 1980s made the transition from software engineer to entrepreneur. "Most of my colleagues went into business. Those who did not are now struggling to survive."

The transition from engineer or researcher to entrepreneur was not as conscious for many as it was for Polushkin, who picked a new field and dived into it. For Vadim Rakhovsky, who headed a defense ministry technical think-tank for over two decades, entry into the world of business was pure accident. In 1990 he was on a flight from Moscow to New York, struggling to sleep despite two inebriated men conducting a loud discussion of lumber shipping problems. "I could not go to sleep to their squealing," recalled Rakhovsky, a man who was clearly used to having his way, with residual outrage. "Finally, I turned to them and said, 'Let's you tell me your problem. I'll solve it, and then we'll go to sleep.' They explained to me that it had become unprofitable to dry timber since fuel prices went up. The solution was plain to see. They were using great amounts of fuel to dry the wood because of the huge difference between the temperature inside and outside the drier. All they had to do was pump out the air, creating a vacuum, causing the temperature at which water boils to fall to 41 degrees Celsius." Soon Rakhovsky signed a contract to develop vacuum lumber-drying chambers.

A bald man in his late fifties who looked more like a mid-level apparatchik than the leader of a think-tank, Rakhovsky liked to complain. I suppose this was in keeping with his social circle's new traditions. He told me that science funding had dropped to zero and that this was a tragedy. He added that in the olden days he had had unlimited access to all sorts of information, including data on secret defense work in the United States. All he had to do was lodge a request, he said, and the next morning the needed formulae and drawings would be on his desk. I was not sure why he was telling me this. Perhaps it was a measure of how much the regime had appreciated his work. Now the Defense Ministry seemed to have all but forgotten about his existence. He may have felt a tad insulted, but the lack of attention from the authorities probably only aided him in transforming the think-tank into Antekh, a research and development firm that developed not only vacuum chambers but vacuum switches, marble furniture veneers, and unbreakable high-class china. Rakhovsky projected the requisite disappointment that his staff were no longer advancing scientific theory, but he also acknowledged with reluctant satisfaction that they lived far better than they could have imagined in Soviet times.

Mark Nemoiter also realized he was becoming a businessman only when the process was already under way. In 1987 thirty-seven-year-old Nemoiter was working at a research institute that developed a software package for the Bulgarian government. When the state allowed the creation of private and semi-private structures as alternatives to state-owned institutions, Nemoiter rushed over to the Ministry of Finance, where his newly formed joint venture specializing in mainframe software for Warsaw Pact countries became number twelve in the new registry of private Russian businesses.

Once he tasted entrepreneurship, Nemoiter started forming new companies and diversifying at a mindboggling rate that just about matched the rate of change in the country. Having at various points marketed software, exported timber, and imported Korean-made telephones and umbrellas, by the mid-1990s he was head of a company that employed about thirty-five people and grossed around $5 million annually. Nemoiter's main lines of business were importing raw materials for the tobacco and food industries and designing and constructing small hydroelectric plants. The former activity, according to Nemoiter, was the most promising line of business in today's Russia by virtue of offering the highest profit margin. The latter was an *idée fixe* of his partner, an engineer who spent two decades attempting to convince gigantism-afflicted Soviet authorities to construct small power plants; now newly independent manufacturers were interested in acquiring their own sources of power, and Nemoiter and Company were poised to fill the niche.

Nemoiter was a true missionary of enterprise, the sort any popularizer of privatization would dream of. Sitting in his office – a gray-carpeted, modular-furnished Western-style oasis in the center of Moscow – the plump, rosy-cheeked Nemoiter looked like a Type A personality in heaven. "My work is so interesting," he boasted. "Every day I have to solve at least five major problems or ten lesser ones. Take, for example, what I went through when we got our first shipment of coconut oil from Singapore. We needed safety certificates. First, we waited our turn with the certificate agency for a week, while I had to pay $200 per container per day for storage. Then they said the radioactivity was ten times the legal maximum. Ten days later, after we appealed, they admitted they'd made a mistake but said the lead content was too high. Finally, they made it clear: certificates cost $1,000 per container – no testing required – or no certificate, regardless of what we actually have in there." All it took was a bribe. "Now I tell you," continued Nemoiter enthusiastically. "No Western businessman has ever dreamed of the kinds of problems we encounter every day."

The obstacles facing entrepreneurs in Russia were legendary. The twenty-two different taxes to be paid. The customs tariffs changing every week. The bureaucracy that daily invented new mechanisms for the simplest procedures. The bribes. The protection rackets. The last could really cramp one's style. Nemoiter, for example, drove a battered Soviet-made Fiat, kept the outside of his summerhouse unpainted, and stayed home most nights in order to avoid drawing more unwanted attention from the Mob, always on the lookout for those who lived as though they had money.

On the whole, though, these entrepreneurs seemed to find the endless difficulty of doing business truly inspiring. They were people accustomed to avoiding confrontation with their oppressor – they had been geniuses at staking out space outside its purview. But they had never expected to be able to bargain their way beyond limitations, to use their considerable mental faculties not to avoid but to overcome obstacles. They relished their problems in a way that allowed them to see themselves as warriors.

"The relationship between the government and the entrepreneurs is best compared to gang rape, except the group being raped is far larger than the group doing the raping." This richly metaphoric description belonged to Ivan Kivelidi, a former journalist who headed up a finance company and the Russian Business Roundtable, an entrepreneurs' association. He added that where the state let up, organized crime turned up the pressure. "But as a result, the Russian entrepreneur compares favorably to his Western counterpart: he is always alert, lean, and in good shape, like a marathon runner."

Such was the trade-off: these people had given up their special social status as the cultural elite in the vague margins of Soviet society in exchange for the self-image of trailblazers, heroes – even (and here is where their intelligentsia heritage made itself known) somewhat self-sacrificing heroes. "In a normal society," said Protasova, "techies will work with computers and whatever else they were trained to do, but we do not live in a normal society, so this is what we have to do." There was a nostalgic note in this statement, tempered by the clear awareness that the sacrifice was well worth the payoff.

"I look at people who stayed in software," said Nemoiter, "and I see: they are making decisions about whether they can buy sausage or good cheese this week. Meanwhile, I make decisions that affect the lives of the thirty-five people who work for me, that affect the fate of my business. All my life I was told I was a cog in the wheel. Only in the last five years have I realized this was not so." Probably the biggest benefit of being a businessman was this uncommon confidence. In a population of people who had seen everything they knew, enjoyed and believed in slip away, this was a small group that felt it had gained – not lost – power. Perhaps this was because, as Abramova would say, they had found a solution – not the one they may have envisioned a few years earlier, but a solution nonetheless.

Intoxicated by this feeling of power, they seemed to feel they could do anything. "I had a realization in October 1993, when I was watching the shelling of Parliament on television," claimed Polushkin. "I realized that the real power is not with the politicians or the masses but with us, the young entrepreneurs." I could easily see where such certainty would come from. Russia continued to be a country where knowledge was strictly rationed. Having insights into the mechanisms of decision-making as well as the personalities of the decision-makers themselves – and entrepreneurs, in their confrontations with the state, had gained that – could make one feel a mere step away from having actual state power.

The militant Kivelidi, being of an older generation, amended Polushkin's statement by dropping the "young" appellation, but his sentiment was the same: "Entrepreneurs will come to rule the country," he said. "It is inevitable."

A few months after he made that statement, Kivelidi was murdered, apparently the victim of a finance deal gone sour. His violent metaphors for the circumstances of Russian entrepreneurship turned out to be even more valid than he may have imagined. Still, his predictions regarding the role of the entrepreneurs in making the new state also proved prescient. As the 1996 presidential campaign unfolded, the entrepreneurs, suddenly aware of the precariousness of their newly earned status, entered the political fray *en masse*. They negotiated with different candidates; they financed and ran campaigns. In the end, an army of recently minted bankers, advertising executives and media moguls – many, if not most, of them former techies – virtually took over Boris Yeltsin's re-election campaign and won it for him through savvy advertising and grand, New-Russian-style campaign gimmicks. They, it could be argued, came to exert a greater influence in government than the members of the intelligentsia who actually became politicians – perhaps because on the new Russian value scale they had not only more to lose but more to offer.

From a distance, this new phenomenon of the educated entrepreneur would seem to bear out the theory, advanced by some scholars, that with time the intelligentsia would give way to a new professional class. The expectation behind this theory dictated that a comfortable enough life would soothe the intelligentsia's passions and help it channel its energies and knowledge into acquiring still more comfort. On closer inspection, though, the New Russians hatched from the old techies appeared very much to embody some of the intelligentsia's longest-standing traditions. They were actively importing and popularizing the ways of the West, from its sartorial fashions to liberal economic thought. And, most important, they assumed a cautious and vigilant posture toward the state, damning it as the enemy and aggressor one day and swooping in to save the status quo the next. Whether by old habit or new exigency, they had created an incarnation of the intelligentsia for the new times.

CHAPTER SEVEN

THE POLITICIANS

Yevgeny Saburov's desk was strewn with objects. Four pipes, tobacco in a pouch, tobacco in a jar, a box of miniature cigars, a box of standard cigars, a desktop lighter, a pipe lighter, a pipe cleaner, a red pack of long More cigarettes with a red disposable lighter, a coffee cup, a box of giant copper paper clips and a little gray hard-rubber toy that looked like two interlocked elongated horseshoes. As we talked, Saburov's meaty freckled hands fiddled with the toy, then with a cigar, a lighter, a pipe, as though performing a convoluted ritual whereby all the objects on the desk were gathered closer and closer to Saburov himself, on a smaller and smaller patch of desk space, and his hands switched between objects faster and faster, until he swept the coffee cup off the desk and into his lap.

He jumped up, sending his black leather armchair, now covered with the light-brown indignity of coffee and milk, rolling into the wall. Holding his arms away from his large body, Saburov looked down at the huge stain on his wrinkled tan chinos, then around the room, as though trying to reconstruct what had landed him in such an embarrassing predicament. Then he called for his secretary, a cheerful short-haired young blonde who generally exhibited all of the helpfulness but none of the deference customary for assistants to top bank officials. "You have been gesticulating again," she admonished her boss. She instructed Saburov to go splash water on the stain in the bathroom, then turned to me in mock despair: "He was waving his arms around, wasn't he?"

In referring to Saburov, his friends generally expressed the befuddled resignation one might feel upon being exposed to a force of nature, albeit a benevolent one. I had heard of Saburov for years; he was known in so many different fields that one might have thought there were several people with the same name. He had served as the deputy minister of education in the Russian government and then as its minister of economics. He had authored the economic program that helped Boris Yeltsin get elected President. Then he moved south to head up the government of the Crimea, Ukraine's tiny but troublesome possession. He was the author of many popular articles on economics published in the leading Russian newspapers. He was also a poet – in fact, one of *the* poets of his generation, one of those whose poems were well-known to poetry readers for two decades before his first book came out in 1995. All this made me imagine him as a post-Soviet Renaissance man, an intense and refined intellectual who could navigate any situation with precision and make himself indispensable in any social group he entered.

I saw Saburov for the first time at the Russian Humanities University, where bearded thin bespectacled Jewish writers led a series of seminars in modern poetry. One of the instructors, a shy, stuttering poet named Mikhail Aisenberg, introduced Saburov as his friend and mentor. Awestruck students, as painfully tense as only twenty-year-olds about to meet an idol can be, waited. Before them appeared a man in a baggy gray suit, possessed of a build and bearing that made him look unkempt even when he had not spilled coffee on himself, with a head of tousled straw-colored hair and with a bushy moustache on a face with so many pockmarks they nearly obscured his features. He sat down, mumbled something, ruffled through his attaché case for an uncomfortably long moment, and then addressed the room in his best lecture voice:

"Aisenberg has probably told you a bit about poetry. Poetry dates back to about the time of Dante. That's when we know that lyrics separated from words to become a separate thing."

He was painfully inappropriate: feeding junior-high truths to a group of inflated young poetic egos. The students retaliated with especially pretentious questions, and he cut them down with such lines as, "If you are going to use ridiculous phrases like 'objective thinking,' there is no point in talking to you at all." He could hardly have made himself more unpopular.

Then he took out an overstuffed black leather Filofax, from which he extracted a filthy little blue-plastic-bound notebook. The students settled in for what they now clearly expected to be a miserable hour of listening to a philistine's attempts at poetry (since at the time his poetry was available only in home-made books, most of them had only heard about it). An hour later the room was filled with that mix of confused but electric emotion that emerges when an artist has succeeded in turning a small part of his audience's world upside down – all the more confused and all the more striking because it was the last thing the audience had come to expect.

Saburov was clearly a man who could succeed only on his merits. He could not endear himself to any group of people because he could not fully belong to any group. He moved from one to another easily enough because he could never comfortably stay; he could only tumble through like – a force of nature. In 1990, when he appeared at Staraya Ploshad, the government compound in the center of Moscow, to report for his first day at work as the Russian deputy minister of education, one of the women guards moved to stop him: untidy men wearing bright red shirts with rolled-up sleeves and a collar opened to reveal a tan hairy chest did not enter the building, much less claim office space there. Another guard quickly contained her overzealous colleague, whispering loudly, "That's the new deputy minister." *Bureaucrats work spectacularly*, Saburov noted with amused satisfaction.

Neither in his wildest dreams nor in his worst nightmares could Saburov have thought he would end up very near the top of one of the world's grandest bureaucracies. Saburov, who grew up in the Crimea, came to Moscow a sixteen-year-old mathematics prodigy in 1962, when the Thaw-era poetry craze was at its zenith. He had been writing consistently since the age of thirteen, though his first poem dated to the year he was six and he suspected he had become a writer even earlier. "Let's say my feelings for mathematics cooled off," he told me, recalling his time at the university. "I was at the age – around twenty or so – when a poet's thinking is shaped. I don't mean his style or his literary manner, which can change in time, but the way he approaches the world."

Saburov was still at that crucially impressionable age when the 1968

Soviet invasion of Czechoslovakia signaled the indisputable end of the era of relative liberalism. "We grew up – " Saburov began, twisting the rubber horseshoe toy, then briefly trailed off, interrupting himself: "No, I shouldn't say that. Everyone thinks that he grew up during the worst period. So we grew up, let's say, during a rather unpleasant period. Co-operation with the regime or anything that smacked of it was unacceptable to me. I never joined the Party. Which meant that was it: all roads were closed off. They even put off placing me in charge of a research group until there came a point when they had no other choice: there was no one else who specialized in my area. And too, they warned me that they could only have a single non-party-member at my institute, so I used up their quota."

Saburov was a member of that generation and that social group that was terrorized from inside by what the poet Sergei Gandlevsky dubbed "the honesty psychosis" – the active obsession with categorizing life choices as honest and dishonest, the endless discussion of the criteria by which honorable people should live in a dishonorable society. "That's all we talked about," said Saburov. "The biggest fear, of course, was the defense industry. Working for defense was dishonest, it was bad and so forth. And there really were people who did not think they were working for the defense and then found out that their work was used that way, and they would be terrified. I witnessed their visits to the late Father Aleksandr Men." Men, the Russian Orthodox priest who was so popular among the intelligentsia was, in essence, one of two people in post-World War II Russia whose voice carried absolute moral weight with its members; the other was Andrei Sakharov. Their words were remembered, quoted and, most important, heeded.

Father Men deplored the life choice made by a part of Saburov's generation to become night-guards or boilermen – minimally paid and minimally useful positions, hence the best places for good citizens of a bad state. As Saburov recalled, Father Men had this to say on the topic: "What if *it* happens tomorrow? And we are told, 'Take the power, stand at the helm, do what you will.' And then what – we will all come out with our brooms?" There were certain places, Saburov understood, that were unsuitable for an honest person; the list was short and etched into every brain that would think itself honorable. "He thought that people should work in their fields and attempt to realize their potential," Saburov recalled. "To approach it from the point of view that the worse everything is the better it is, because that means this system will collapse soon – that is even more unethical than going and working someplace."

Saburov went to work as an economist, specializing, at different times, in the economics of residential construction, of education and of the chemical industry. By the time perestroika began, he was working in macroeconomic theory. He was not a career man – and this too was a sign of the times. "One could work in one's narrow discipline, but as soon as you reached a level of having to participate in any more or less significant decisions, you encountered the sort of mental decay that prevented functioning." So he toiled away in the area of economics that attracted him most, wrote poetry and a couple of novels and a play, and cracked endless jokes about all the absurdities of the Soviet system that he observed in his working life.

The first time I saw Galina Starovoitova I could not see her at all. It was March 1991, a time that journalists and others who are inspired by public events still remember as magical, possibly the most exciting that ever was. Gorbachev's reforms had taken hold; the country even seemed accustomed to having a liberated press and to the concept of free elections. But now Gorbachev seemed to be back-pedaling, while the democrats were pushing for more – and the whole of Russia seemed to be behind them. The Democratic Russia movement, a popular front that could draw hundreds of thousands to the streets, was backing Boris Yeltsin as its candidate in the first Russian presidential election, scheduled for June. In March Gorbachev, apparently frightened by the loosening of his grip on the country, banned public demonstrations in Moscow. A few days later defiant Muscovites came out for what was possibly the largest independent peaceful demonstration in all of Russian history.

After ten years of living as an *émigrée*, I had been back in Moscow for just a few days. I was lucky enough to be staying in the very center of town, a block from the square for which the demonstration had been set. That part of Moscow, filled with Stalinist-style buildings with three-story archways facing eight-lane roads, imposes a superhuman scale, enough to dwarf, it seems, any gathering of people. But this time the human mass overwhelmed the city center, plugging up all its entrances and exits. I had to invent a snaking path, through courtyards and cracks between buildings, so that I could finally join the crowd about a mile from the speaker. I could discern the passionate pattern of the woman's speech but no words. Every so often the crowd, rocking from block to block, chanted, "Yel-tsin! Yel-tsin!" As I pushed forward through the endless rows of people, I asked who was speaking. Starovoitova. Of course, I never managed to see her that day.

Five years later Starovoitova recalled her 1991 self with a sort of detached amazement that bordered on awe. "I could step forward firmly, with certainty, and lead large groups of people, speak at rallies of half a million people," she marveled over lunch in the Russian Parliament's opulent dining room. "Often there were tanks in the streets, whether in Yerevan or in Moscow or in Petersburg, and I felt no fear. Now, in hindsight, I realize how little it would have taken to stage some sort of provocation at that time, to have one of us shot. To have the crowd trample us and then present it as an accident. Later my friends and I discussed how easy that would have been to do, to create an incident that would have crushed many people. Imagine the square in front of the Kremlin where we often held demonstrations. We would always speak from this place between columns, and the crowd would be facing us, and there were times it was 700,000 strong, packed in tight. Right above the spot where we usually stood there is a balcony that no one ever guarded. All someone would have had to do is throw, say, a can with some burning gasoline down there – and there would have been several dozen dead. They could have thrown a cat off that balcony – "

Five years later, she was still trying to make sense of the sequence of events, actions and emotions that yanked her, a rank-and-file researcher at one of Russia's many academic institutes, out of an obscure and measured life and thrust her into the power elite. Like Saburov, Galina Starovoitova was born in 1946, glimpsed the tail of the Thaw, and, having barely known the public outside, retreated into a private universe that was as honest as she could make it. At the age of twenty-two she signed a group letter protesting the Soviet invasion of Czechoslovakia and was immediately treated to the niceties of the secret police system, complete with an interrogation at the St Petersburg KGB headquarters. Soon she became pregnant, stalling trouble and allowing herself to find refuge at home. She became a kitchen dissident, or, as it was sometimes called, an "internal émigrée," someone whose convictions compelled her to abandon the country – but without leaving it physically.

At college Starovoitova studied social psychology. Later she became interested in ethnic issues and did her PhD in anthropology. By the mid 1980s she had traveled the honest person's path to success: she was a highly respected specialist in a very narrow discipline, and this was virtually the only level on which she engaged the society in which she lived. Starovoitova was studying the ethnic psychology of very old Caucasus residents. Every summer she was off for months of field research; three of those summers she spent in Nagorny Karabakh, a tiny Armenian exclave in the southern republic of Azerbaijan.

On February 12, 1988, the local governing body of Nagorny Karabakh voted to secede from Azerbaijan in order to join Armenia. In the years to come small regions all over Eastern Europe would struggle, one after another, to draw the world's attention to their plight, their territorial history and their particular memory of oppression and violence. More often than not, these calls for justice, coming on a wave of democratic transformation, would lead to more violence, more blood and pain, revitalizing the seventy-year-old term "Balkanization." But long before the Balkans erupted, there was Nagorny Karabakh.

The Karabakh declaration led to mass demonstrations in Armenia in support of the region and similarly numerous anti-Armenian rallies in Azerbaijan. Later, there would be fully-fledged modern-day pogroms, with dozens and possibly hundreds of ethnic Armenians slaughtered throughout Azerbaijan. Then there would be an all-out war. In 1988, the Gorbachev administration, apparently vaguely aware of the looming bloodshed, reacted with an anxious admixture of demagoguery, threats, pleas for compromise, administrative and financial palliatives, and arrests. Journalists and anthropologists were searching every map in vain, trying to locate the tiny epicenter of ethnic tension in the giant empire.

Starovoitova knew exactly where this place was. She knew every village in Nagorny Karabakh by touch, by smell, by heart. The words coming across in the news reports echoed for her with the history of the land told in the voices of people she knew well.

There is a very particular taste of helplessness that fills the mouths of the Russian intelligentsia like a silent scream when an outrage rips through a part of the empire. At times like these the carefully maintained distance from the government, the skillfully crafted separate world of the intelligentsia, seem like protective chambers of powerlessness.

Starovoitova, who felt such an intimate connection to the events in Nagorny Karabakh, felt more absurdly powerless than the average guilt-ridden intellectual, because, having slipped on ice days earlier, she was just then bedridden with a broken right leg and a broken left arm. Starovoitova did literally the only thing she could: she wrote a letter. It was a personal letter addressed to friends and colleagues in Armenia. "I simply expressed my understanding of the issue," Starovoitova told me, "and said that I envied their people the courage and solidarity that it had shown face-to-face with history – because my people, the Russians, were no longer or not yet capable of that sort of solidarity."

For Starovoitova's Armenian friends, their most intimate passions were now driving hundreds of thousands of demonstrators. So it was only natural that they took their friend's letter and made copies. Enough for everyone – about 100,000. They handed them out in the square in Yerevan, the Armenian capital, where the people were demonstrating.

"The last line that I had put in this letter when I typed it in bed was my home telephone number and my address," said Starovoitova. "And people started to call, hundreds of Armenians whom I did not know, every two or three minutes, day and night, with words and tears of gratitude. They would say, 'We have been so hurt by the Moscow regime, but you understand us, you are a Russian daughter of the

Armenian people, we thank you for that, you are like [the poet] Valery Briusov and all others who helped Armenians during the Turkish genocide of 1915.' There were very overstated comparisons, very beautiful but very sincere words – Armenians have always been very sensitive to those non-Armenians who share their pain, who understand them. And that's how it was that overnight I became known to all of Armenia. It was because of this letter. Without my knowledge it was broadcast over Radio Liberty. The director of my institute now wanted me to leave because my position contradicted the line of the Party and of the government. And by this time I did not care – I thought I had done the right thing. This was all unexpected, it was a shock, but I was not at all afraid of the authorities' reaction."

A lot of forces came together to make Starovoitova a suddenly formidable political figure: her unique relationship to the events, a desperate need for allies and new leaders, a paradoxical but still unselfconscious need to idolize representatives of the Russian "center." Starovoitova herself was primed for taking the step – rather, a leap – into the political fray. She was a member of several political discussion clubs, the perestroika-era public offspring of the intelligentsia kitchens. She had been elected cochair of the best-known of them, the *Moscow Tribune*, whose open-ended meetings drew the most articulate liberal thinkers in Moscow. Another cochair was Andrei Sakharov, who gave Starovoitova his steady support and, no doubt, inspiration, as she was catapulted to political fame.

In 1989 the people of Armenia elected Galina Starovoitova to the Supreme Soviet of the USSR. There was a kind of electoral logic in this: who better to represent the interests of Armenians in the "center" than an ally in that center? Plus, most of the most popular Armenian leaders had been jailed in connection with the events in Nagorny Karabakh. She immediately joined the Interregional Deputies Group, the relatively small but vocal faction headed, among others, by Sakharov and Boris Yeltsin, that stood up to the overwhelming Communist majority in the Supreme Soviet. In 1990 her native city of Leningrad elected her to the Supreme Soviet of Russia. She was a leader of Democratic Russia, the largest popular movement of the era. In 1991 she became President

Yeltsin's adviser on interethnic issues. She was one of the most famous and most popular politicians in Russia. •

In 1988 Yevgeny Saburov received a call from an education official who remembered him from Saburov's days as an education economist. Education reform was emerging as one of the most important agenda items of the Gorbachev era, and this official wanted Saburov to draft an economic proposal. "There were interesting people then among those teachers involved in reform," remembered Saburov. "They were always holding their conferences, and they started inviting me, because, I think, there were about five people in the country who specialized in the economics of education. I drew in the rest of them, and we started getting some money for our work. This was quite important, to be honest, because we were very poor. It's hard to fathom now how poor we were." Saburov helped work out proposals that would change the system of financing for secondary schools, taking, at least in theory, some leverage away from bureaucrats and giving it to parents. While this scheme was being tested in several school districts, Saburov became well known among education professionals.

In 1990, following the first more or less free election to the Supreme Soviet of the Russian Federation (the election was governed by transitional laws that limited individual participation in favor of organizations, so it was far from a one person one vote ideal), a new government, the Soviet of Ministers of the Russian Federation, was formed. The guiding principle for the newly democratic times was to draw government members not from the ranks of party functionaries, as had always been done before, but from among successful and well-respected professionals in the fields represented in the cabinet. Eduard Dneprov, an education scholar and a leader of the education reform movement, was chosen as minister of education. He called Saburov and, as the economist later recalled, said, "I won't be able to accomplish anything unless I make you my deputy for economics." Saburov laughed. What had started as a professional lark less than two years earlier was turning entirely too serious. He was prepared to file Dneprov's offer away as nothing more than a funny anecdote.

"That day was Pavel Men's, Father Aleksandr's brother's, nameday," a day that celebrates a Russian Orthodox saint for whom one is named. "I went to his house and told him about Dneprov's call because I thought it made a funny story. Suddenly Pavel got this absolutely grim expression on and said, 'You know, this is that very moment when we can do something.' I didn't really· understand what he meant. The next day I was visiting Mikhail Aisenberg and started telling him the story too. And I told him that Pavel had just been floored. And Misha got this strange expression too and said, 'You know, Pavel is probably right, you should accept this offer.' All this was so fantastic, so impossible to grasp, that I just decided that they were both equally wrong and I shouldn't listen to anyone anyway." Apparently, however, he did listen, because after being worked over by all of his teacher acquaintances and some members of the government, Saburov became deputy minister of education of the Russian Federation.

The revolutions that transformed the Eastern Bloc in 1989–91 were largely the work of people who found themselves thrust into positions of great power and authority by the forces that Gorbachev-era reforms had unleashed. Once in the government, Saburov too was suddenly near the center of the force that was echoing throughout the Soviet Union and the disintegrating Eastern Bloc. A number of political newcomers all over this region were pondering the no longer theoretical questions of the decade: How would property relationships change in the countries that sought to change themselves? Should state property be privatized through give-aways, through vouchers, or for money? Should economic reform follow a "shock therapy" or a gradual model? In this ecstatic moment of theory about to transform practice, Saburov too developed his own ideas and presented them to the government when the opportunity presented itself. Thus in April 1991 he was appointed head of a working group drafting the Russian government's program of economic reform. In August 1991 Saburov became the minister of economics in the government of the Russian Federation.

If Saburov experienced his own speedy political ascent as something of an absurdity, he saw the phenomenon itself – the poet-politician – as logical and even traditional. To his mind, politicians and poets were made of the same cloth. One of his favorite theories concerned the modes of thinking employed by different sorts of people. "When a scientist sees a chair," he explained, "he sees its essence, and he sees it as a piece of furniture, representative of a kind that is called 'chairs.' When a poet sees a chair, he sees only that particular chair. He might observe that it is, say, of bent wood, or that it's a Viennese-back chair, he may see the light as it falls on it, or the color of the wood, but he does not extrapolate." Scientists, he said, engage in 'essential' thinking. Poets think 'existentially.' So do politicians. Running down a long list of poet-politicians, including Fyodor Tiutchev and Pierre Augustin de Beaumarchais, Saburov explained that politicians, like poets, were called upon to react to particular events in particular ways.

The particular events that occupied the Russian government in 1990–91 were congresses, elections, reorganizations of the government, a *coup d'état* – anything but long-range economic reform. Papers crawled through the bureaucratic maze at the speed of a snail while outside the government building history broke the sound barrier. Saburov and his colleagues looked on in horror as the Russian economy collapsed and their best-written plans turned into scrap paper. Meanwhile, after the failed August 1991 coup they were presented with the most daunting economic problem of their entire career, possibly the economic question of the century: how to engineer the divorce of fifteen republics of the Soviet Union, all of which had for decades been inextricably tied to Moscow.

A group of economists, including Saburov and future liberal political leader Grigory Yavlinsky, advocated a political division with a good deal of economic unity, followed, perhaps, by a gradual and carefully negotiated division of economic property. For months they worked on treaties, which were then signed by all Soviet member-governments. But the tidal wave of change, helped along by the personal and political ambitions of a great many people, once again swept away the plans and the treaties and, this time, Saburov himself. The political will to take apart the Soviet Union to its very foundation immediately, with no gradual plans that were perceived as wishy-washy, was too powerful. Saburov fell victim to a banal palace intrigue propelled by this political *force majeure*. After three months of negotiating treaties and agreements that would facilitate the gradual economic separation of the Soviet Union's member republics, Saburov was accused of attempting to stall change. On November 6, 1991, during Saburov's wife's birthday party, one of the guests, an economist named Yegor Gaidar, apologetically informed the hosts that he had just been appointed to replace Saburov as the minister of economics. Saburov's wife, fed up with the unglamorous life of politics, said she could not have wished for a better present.

It stands to reason that Galina Starovoitova learned of her own retirement from the same source: the highest-placed intelligentsia member in the government. On November 3, 1992, an aide to Gaidar, who was then serving as prime minister, called Starovoitova to warn her that the President had signed a decree removing her from her post. Starovoitova had been expecting it. The conflict between the President and the reactionary Supreme Soviet was at a high point. The threat of impeachment by a vote of the Supreme Soviet seemed formidable. President Yeltsin was apparently preparing to jettison some of the high-profile democrats in his administration in an attempt to pacify the rebellious Parliament. Eventually nearly all of the first wave of democrats in the government, including Gaidar himself, would be sacrificed.

Starovoitova was especially vulnerable because she was immensely unpopular with the old-school regional leaders and the military establishment. A minority organization within the armed forces, called Soldiers for Democracy, was lobbying to have Starovoitova named defense minister; the suggestion that the military might be led not only by a civilian but by a woman gravely offended the sensibilities of most military officials. Nor was Starovoitova known for her team spirit and diplomatic skills. The journalist Oleg Poptsov, then the head of Russian State Television, characterized her as "being on the team but allowing herself to comment on the qualities of the team's members whenever she pleased, wherever she pleased, and however much she pleased."

Starting in the spring of 1992 Yeltsin began to put distance between himself and Starovoitova, who had been one of his closest advisers. In the fall, when fighting broke out on the border of the Russian Federation's Caucasian republics of North Ossetia and Ingushetia – a harbinger of the bloodshed that would occur in the northern Caucasus in the coming years – Starovoitova was unable even to get the President's ear. Instead, as she learned later, the President of North Ossetia was able to get through to Yeltsin and pressure him finally into removing Starovoitova.

If Starovoitova fostered the illusion that she had become a part of the political establishment, the way the establishment spat her out proved just how accidental her presence had been. I heard her tell the story of her removal several times; it was a well-memorized list of grievances that seemed to pain Starovoitova years later. "I had become a member of the new political elite, and Yeltsin knew the rules of the *nomenklatura* game very well," she told me. "By tradition when someone was removed, a reason was always given, something that spared the person's self-esteem. Even in the cases of people whose rank was much lower than mine they were usually allowed to maintain their government medical care, keep their bodyguards, the car and other benefits – until they were given their next appointment or, in some cases, indefinitely. This time, they took away my car, my security staff and everything in the space of two hours. I was the only woman in the administration, so one might expect that they would have shown more concern for my welfare, but all the Communists – and all these apparatchiks were still Communists – were just too happy to dance on my bones."

The vastly telling body of Soviet apparatchik jargon termed people "human material." In just three years Starovoitova completed the journey from feeling like a cog in the Soviet scholarly wheel to being perceived suddenly as indispensable – first by her constituents, then by the President himself – and to being disposed of as used-up human material. Writing at the time, Poptsov summed up Starovoitova's experience this way: "She had thought that she was intended to create a new philosophy, but [the President] needed something else: someone simply to wash the windows in the house, the better to see what was going on outside." For a century and a half the intelligentsia had longed for an opportunity to enlighten the government. Starovoitova, Saburov and several others lived in an era when the state finally called on the intelligentsia to enlighten it. The problem, as it turned out, was that the intelligentsia perceived enlightenment as changing thought processes and the state's relationship to its citizens; the state, on the other hand, simply sought information that would aid it in perpetuating itself.

Within four days of her ousting, Starovoitova was on a plane to the United States. "The Russian Research Center at Harvard University had been asking me to come for a while, and I had been saying I didn't have the time," she recalled. "So they called and said, 'Maybe you'll have the time now?' I was so grateful to America for pulling me out of this morally devastating situation." Later, when Yegor Gaidar was removed from the government and given a new research institute as a consolation prize, he invited Starovoitova to shape her own project there. "He knows nothing about ethnography, so this was more of a friendly gesture to help me find a place." Starovoitova gratefully accepted this bit of intelligentsia solidarity and formed an ethnography studies laboratory, which functioned at Gaidar's institute until Starovoitova re-entered politics in 1996.

Thank God for research institutes, the last safe haven for the intelligentsia. Saburov too found a quiet but stimulating research position, heading an analytical center that produced white papers for the Russian government. He watched in horror as Gaidar pursued his "shock therapy" reforms – both because he thought this approach wrong and because he predicted that the actions that made Gaidar so unpopular in the country would also discredit the concept of the intelligentsia in government. In another four years, when President Yeltsin swept the last of the liberal intelligentsia out of his government, achieving breathtaking apparatchik homogeneity, he would prove Saburov's prediction right. But before this happened, while the idea of liberal thinkers at the helm still had currency, Saburov would get a second chance to express his poetic self politically.

In 1993 and 1994 another conflict was brewing amid the ruins of the empire. When the Soviet Union disintegrated, the Crimea, a Black Sea resort area favored by Russian and Soviet rulers, became part of the independent state of Ukraine. But not only was the overwhelming majority of its population ethnic Russians, not only had it belonged to the Russian republic of the USSR until the 1950s, it was also a place of unique strategic and sentimental importance. It contained the city built around the centuries-old fortress of Sevastopol, and it housed the elite Black Sea Fleet, also an object of dispute. And it cradled the most romantic and treasured memories of a great many Russians, especially those who had ever enjoyed privilege. Yevgeny Saburov had been born there.

By 1994 the Ukrainian–Russian dispute – rather, the on-again, off-again efforts alternately to stoke and to put out the Crimean fire – had produced another tiny area that was virtually autonomous. It had its own parliament, its own president and, for a time, its own significant measure of freedom of action, owing to its leverage on the post-Soviet international scene. The President of the Crimea, Yuri Meshkov, invited Yevgeny Saburov to become his prime minister. Saburov grabbed several colleagues willing to go along for the experience, and set off for his native foreign land.

The following six months offered more of those particular events to which poet-politicians must react in particular ways than Saburov could have imagined. There was the cholera epidemic, for example, when Saburov had to mobilize the military to get all the garbage out of the cities and to create a makeshift sanatorium for the city's homeless in an old Young Pioneer camp. That was one of the few things Saburov managed to pull off. He also got the local budget in working order, making sure salaries were paid on time. But for a prime minister imported to institute reform, he was a study in unproductiveness.

"I encountered an entirely unexpected situation," he told me. "Meshkov turned out to be not only inexperienced but – " he paused, as did his hands. "I had been through it all in Russia – when an inexperienced leader takes on a crazy task. He is immediately surrounded by con artists. The inexperienced leader is always wanting a miracle. Meshkov was always convinced that he was about to get $10 billion or $40 billion.

We kept trying to explain to him those amounts of available currency simply do not exist. Then he started to hide what he was doing from us. He would secretly travel to Switzerland. Meanwhile, he was stonewalling reform. It was Russia of five years earlier all over again."

Meanwhile Saburov himself became the object of vicious attack before he even set foot in the Crimea, while he was still on his way. In his zeal to help his native land, Saburov was apparently oblivious to his outward appearance as a Russian politician in disfavor attempting to ply his wares on the outskirts of the empire. Worse, he was as foreign to this land of bureaucratic luxury as any man could be – too educated and, it seems, too principled: principles have little to contribute to the efficient barter world of local politics. Unaware as usual of the obstacles that surrounded him, Saburov stumbled badly at every step.

Before agreeing to speak with me, Saburov set one condition: nothing about the Crimea – if that is what I wanted to talk about, he wanted nothing to do with it. He did talk about it with me in the end, even saying it helped him finally to wrap his mind around the six-month-long nightmare – but he had had an almost panicked fear of dredging up the memories. "What I experienced there was constant lying, constant set-ups, constant eavesdropping and denunciations. Every night I would hear myself libeled on television, and never was I allowed to speak myself. At one point they decided to say that I was a drunk, and I was deluged with invitations to this or that collective farm, with a sit-down dinner every time. And I was clueless as to why they were so hospitable all of a sudden, and I would accept the invitations. And you can imagine what those people talk about among themselves – but I would go and then hear that I had been drinking. Meanwhile, not only do I not like to drink but I have tended toward excess weight my whole life, I have always wanted to lose weight, and here I was being fed for slaughter."

At other times Saburov was accused of embezzling or of trying to benefit from certain privatization schemes. When an investigation showed an accusation to be false, it would be replaced by another. Add to that constant threats to the safety of Saburov, his wife and two daughters. "I was informed that certain representatives of certain countries were negotiating with Crimean organized crime groups regarding the possibility of getting rid of me. Surveillance, libel and threats against me, my family and those members of the government who had come with me – all this was with us at all times." Saburov said he attempted to leave after a month on the job, when it was already clear he would be able to contribute little to the Crimea. For six months Meshkov was able to keep talking Saburov into staying. In addition, the people who came with Saburov often enjoyed their first taste of government work beyond measure – a phenomenon Saburov had observed in his days in the Russian government.

"I learned that power seems very sweet to a lot of people. And having power can really have an impact on a person's psyche – the first time I saw it, with Dneprov, it was a life-shattering discovery for me. After a person is appointed to a high post, something strange starts to happen to him. People whose ambitions lie in other areas do not experience this. What saved me was that poetry was the main thing for me. But people for whom a government post was the high point of their careers would lose all sorts of perspective – even though in terms of personal success, the government is not at all a good place to be. It leaves you no time to think."

Six months after arriving, Yevgeny Saburov left the Crimea for Moscow again. A few months later Yuri Meshkov was stripped of his power by a rebellious parliament and, besieged by threats on his life, disappeared from view.

It took me a few minutes to find on the map the name of the street Saburov had given me. I had been to many similar office buildings that seemed to have appeared on the Moscow landscape overnight. They were not too far from the center of town but always tucked away on some under-inhabited street. They looked conspicuously modern and shiny, once you managed to find them. Behind the parking-lot fence, there was a world very different from the rest of Moscow, with polite security guards, quiet elevators, air conditioning, and secretaries that brought tea in cups of delicate white china.

Saburov's secretary, the cheerful blonde, placed the tea leaves in the cups and poured water on top. Saburov rummaged in a bookcase for a can of condensed milk that he was sure he had stashed there. In addition to the milk, the bookcase contained a hideous doll made of a coconut and several overstuffed binders, including one with a yellowed label with CRIMEA scrawled on it in red marker. Saburov fit in as badly in a corner office in a mirrors-and-steel office building as he did anywhere else. But he seemed quite comfortable. Since returning from the Crimea he had been heading up this small research group within a large Russian bank.

"When I returned, I faced a sort of dilemma," he recalled. "I had either to become an instantly active participant not so much in the economic as in the political process, or I had to make my exit." There were vague offers from the government, but the new prime minister, Victor Chernomyrdin, was rumored to oppose Saburov's return. An attempt to return to the presidential research institute also failed. The management of Menatep Bank, whom Saburov had known in his days in the government, asked him to head a research group within the bank. "I accepted their invitation because I had decided at one point that one can only hold a state position until a certain age. If a person over fifty still occupies a government post, then either he is stealing or he has no real abilities."

Proffered a couple of months after Saburov's fiftieth birthday, this statement seemed equal parts retrospective rationalization and the assessment of a man generally quite pleased with the path his life had taken. Saburov, he himself seemed to think, had come perilously close to the seductive essence of power. "What saved me was that the most important thing in my life is poetry," he repeated. Now that he was apart from the government, he once again had time to think. His first published poetry collection had just been released.

The painful drop from grace and prominence inflicted upon Starovoitova seemed, for a while, to sour her on politics. For two and a half years she spent most of her time in the United States, lecturing at the prestigious Brown University and, under the auspices of the Institute for Peace Studies, writing about interethnic politics. In December 1993 she decided not to try her luck at the election to the new Russian Parliament, remaining in America to work on a book.

Back in Russia, the days of mass interest in politics ended. The Democratic Russia movement, a tiny shadow of its former self, was ripped apart by struggles among its several ambitious leaders. Speaking to me in early 1995, one of its former cochairs, the chemist cum politician Ilya Zaslavsky, said, "The situation is tragic for anyone who came to politics in 1988, as I did, because I saw this as a truly popular political surge. That was a great age, and that age created Democratic Russia. For all of us, Democratic Russia is something dear; it means rallies of half a million people."

Perhaps because she was in the United States, or maybe because she had spoken to those mass rallies so often, Starovoitova seemed to hold on to that vision of politics longer than most others. Through the spring of 1995 she maintained a foot-in-the-door policy, returning to Russia regularly to chair ever-dwindling Democratic Russia congresses. Finally, in the autumn of 1995, she took the plunge again. In a parliamentary election in which the democrats fared worse than ever since Russia became an independent state, Starovoitova managed to beat twenty-two candidates for a district seat in the lower house of Parliament. Soon, she launched a campaign for the presidency, putting on a spectacular, if brief, show as the only woman in a crowded field of men. In the end, however, she failed to gather the signatures necessary to get on the ballot.

This seemed symbolic. Starovoitova would probably never again break into the highest level of politics, always falling one step behind the men and the professional apparatchiks. She would almost certainly never again gather an audience of 500,000 or even 5,000. And still, she could not stop. The couple of years of doing scholarly work in unfamiliar comfort only affirmed Starovoitova's commitment to feeding her addiction to politics.

A few days after the end of the 1996 presidential election, Starovoitova was in the hospital, probably in no small part because of overworking. Calling me from her hospital bed, she was attempting to explain the passion. "Politics has become my profession, and nothing else is as interesting," she said. "Scholarship is contemplation of life, but it is not life itself. Politics is about not watching but doing. It is real living."

The next morning she called again. She was going into surgery in a few minutes, she said, but there was an image she wanted to share. "There is an ancient Greek legend about harpies," she told me. "They are shadows that can come to life only if they drink human blood. The life of a scholar is the life of a shadow. When one participates in making the future happen, even a small part of the future – and this is what politics is about – that is when one who is a shadow can come to life. But of course one has to drink blood, including one's own."

CHAPTER EIGHT

THE GOVERNORS

in building a city, they build not a city
but a monument to their own aloneness.
. . .

A land of hyperbole lies beneath them
as the sky of metaphors sails above us.
— Joseph Brodsky

Russia, as Russians are fond of saying, is a very large country. One-sixth of the world's land mass. Unfathomable. Unruly. A person cannot but feel tiny in such a vast place. Even a person in government, even a minister or an adviser to the President, will feel like a cog in a giant wheel. Whatever the intellectual-politicians may have thought in their most euphoric moments, they would eventually be convinced that the intelligentsia will never come significantly to alter the gigantic rusty machine of Russian government.

But Russia is a large country. Far away from Moscow, under the bright sun in the Caucasus mountains, in a place, in fact, that did not legally belong to Russia but considered itself a part of it nonetheless, there was a sleepy college town that fought a bloody war to draw a line between itself and the outside world and turned to its intelligentsia to take it to statehood. The university rector, a historian, became the head of state. A philosopher was in charge of writing laws. A mathematician was mapping foreign policy. The lines between theory and practice dissolved in the heat of an open-ended experiment where history was learned in the streets and philosophy was battled out in Parliament.

Perched at the northern edge of Georgia, pressed tight up against the

Russian border, South Ossetia had a long and embattled history of the sort that breeds wounded pride and uncompromising patriotism. The Ossetians trace their roots in Europe to the first century, a time before there was a Georgia or a Russia, when the Farsi-speaking Alans, who would later become known as the Ossetians, settled in the north of the Caucasus mountains (for the sake of fairness, it should be noted here that many small Caucasian nations claim to be the direct descendants of the Alans, though some hold that these distinguished ancestors spoke a language other than Farsi). Through centuries of war and occupation, the Ossetians were split into two parts: the North, which belonged to Russia, and the South, which was a part of Georgia. In 1801, when Georgia joined the Russian empire, the two halves were reunited. But in 1920, Solomonic justice was restored when Ossetia was formalized as two separate jurisdictions: the North Ossetian Autonomous Republic within Russia and the South Ossetian Autonomous Region within the Soviet Republic of Georgia. South Ossetia, measuring 15,000 square miles, consisted of a city called Tskhinval and several small towns and villages that dotted the Ossetian Military Highway, the beauty of which was made famous by several Ossetian and Russian poets, including Mikhail Lermontov; it runs across the Caucasus mountains to the Russian–Georgian border, where North Ossetia begins.

Like many small peoples, the South Ossetians, who in the 1990s numbered about 70,000, led a less than idyllic existence under the Soviets. Unlike some ethnic groups – the neighboring Chechens, for example – they were allowed to stay on land they considered their own. But between 1934 and 1956, the South Ossetians were subjected to ideological "cleansing" an extraordinary six times. As with many Stalinist purges throughout the Soviet Union, each time the intelligentsia – the keeper of national tradition and pride – was singled out, with whole layers of the population executed, imprisoned, or sentenced to a long term in exile. This helped to raise the intelligentsia's standing in the South Ossetian culture ever higher. One of the South Ossetian martyrs was the rector of the South Ossetian Pedagogical Institute – now the South Ossetian University – who was executed in 1937; his wife, also a teacher, spent fifteen years in Soviet prisons.

Paradoxically, at the same time, the intelligentsia kept regenerating, thanks to the Soviet system for maintaining the appearance of cultural diversity. Like other so-called "autonomous regions," South Ossetia was granted the trappings of limited independence: a local governing body, a pedagogical institute, a research institute charged with studying South Ossetian culture and history, and admission quotas to the main Russian universities. At its peak, the research institute housed 350 researchers who studied the South Ossetians' extraordinarily long recorded history, carefully writing their way around such banned topics as the Stalin purges. The pedagogical institute – though it was as poorly equipped and little respected by academics and even its own students as other provincial Soviet colleges – provided a focal point for the region's patriotism. A history of the institution published on its fiftieth anniversary in 1982 began with a quote from a Tskhinval elder: "When passing the building of the pedagogical institute, every resident of South Ossetia must bow to it as to a temple." Every third resident of South Ossetia had been educated at the institute. The largest structure in the Tskhinval of the 1990s was the unfinished new building complex that was once meant to house the institute and its dormitories. Of Tskhinval's peacetime population of 50,000, about 12,000 people were either students or teachers of the pedagogical institute or the branch of the State Polytechnic Institute located here, or staff members at the research institute. The creative intelligentsia, according to official measures, was also richly represented: the city boasted upward of 200 members of the Soviet Union's exclusive writers', artists' and composers' unions. Though the education privileges the South Ossetians enjoyed were not unique, the region's small population made the percentage of residents who benefited from them unusually high. Most people one met in Tskhinval, it seemed, had an advanced degree – or several. This may not have made South Ossetia any more enlightened and cosmopolitan a place than any other part of the Caucasus, but it did add to its unique air. It was an intellectual ethnic enclave, a university town proud of its little world – and willing to defend it if need be.

In 1990, as the Soviet Union neared collapse and nationalists with Zviad Gamsakhurdia at the helm came to power in Georgia – soon to become its own country and South Ossetia's lone legal guardian – the enclave's limited independence, as well as its relationship with its northern counterpart, lay in peril. As rhetoric glorifying a "Georgia for the Georgians" reached a militaristic pitch, South Ossetians – led by a group of young nationalist intellectuals very close in spirit to leaders that emerged throughout the former Eastern Bloc in the late 1980s – declared a republic, renamed their pedagogical institute a university (to underscore the spirit of independence, for only full-fledged capitals had universities in Soviet times), elected a parliament and began preparing for war. Young men – most of them students at the pedagogical institute – sold their cars and other prized possessions, pooled their resources, and imported all the submachine guns and grenade launchers their roubles could buy. When in January 1991 Georgia sent in what it claims were police troops to cool the passion – and what South Ossetians say were gangs of nationalist soldiers – they encountered a partially armed force of students led by teachers and artists, and a war began, with each side claiming to have been the target of the opening shot. In twenty days, using the university as "a bastion, a Bastille, of sorts," in the words of rector cum president Ludvig Chibirov, the South Ossetians forced the Georgian troops out of Tskhinval and onto the mountains that completely surround the city, which enabled the Georgians to subject Tskhinval to shelling and sniper fire for much of the following eighteen months. In July 1992, after over 500 South Ossetians had died, peacekeeping forces made up of Russian, Georgian and South Ossetian troops entered the city, ensuring a tentative cease-fire.

South Ossetia entered a condition somewhere between war and peace, statehood and obscurity. The land, which considered itself a republic, was officially recognized only by other breakaway regions. The Georgian administration, in both rhetoric and budgeting, largely ignored the existence of South Ossetia and the South Ossetians. In the resulting vacuum, the South Ossetians used Russian roubles as their currency, set their clocks, inexplicably, five minutes behind Georgian – and Russian – time, and got on with the work of mourning their dead, patching up their houses, holding elections and otherwise trying to write their own history.

*

"I never thought I'd see history first-hand," confessed the polyester-clad former biology teacher who, in his capacity as director of the Information Ministry's press center, had the unenviable task of leading me around Tskhinval under the scorching late-May sun in 1994. He fell quiet, hanging his balding head as he considered the distinctly unglamorous spectacle that history turned out to be up-close. Neither the leaders' knowledge of history nor the South Ossetians' love of it – this was a place where kiosks stocked Herodotus (who mentions the Alans) along-side cans of beer – seemed to have prepared them for the untidy and uncontrollable ways in which history writes itself. The historians-turned-lawmakers were only beginning to learn that they could no longer obliterate national tragedy with the stroke of a pen.

Tragedy descended on South Ossetia in triplicate, leaving a trail of debris behind. The beginning of the war was followed in short order by an earthquake that made two snow-covered Caucasian mountains come together, dumping enough excess snow into the narrow mountain rivers to create a devastating flood. Though the war was almost entirely limited to Tskhinval, in the space of a couple of years most of South Ossetia was destroyed by one *force majeure* or another. Some places, the only structures left standing were the ones built to last forever: monuments to Communist leaders.

What used to be the town of Java, South Ossetia's second-largest population center, was now a dusty land of old foundations punctuated with protruding granite monuments: a head of Lenin here, a head of native son Stalin there. Impaled on giant granite columns, they looked more like trophies than tributes, but the symbolism was hardly misplaced: in an era of disaster, the battered population was once again seeing old Communist ideals as beacons of hope.

In a spacious office in Tskhinval's pockmarked (from shelling), charred (from an unrelated fire in 1993) and damp and partially incapacitated (from the resulting water damage) Parliament building, Fatima Pukhayeva, an old Communist Party hand and the person in charge of the South Ossetian education system for the last fourteen years – which now made her a minister – was enthusiastically imparting to me her vision of history. "We had ideology," boomed the extraordinarily imposing woman. "We thought that somebody, somewhere was building Communism. Somebody, somewhere was thinking of us, so we were socially secure. We didn't participate in it personally." In the new times, as the Soviet Union was collapsing, South Ossetians embraced political participation with the enthusiasm of many liberated and threatened small populations and elected a group of young nationalist-democratically minded intellectuals − artists, mathematicians and teachers − to make independence. "And then − look: the end of the world − natural disaster and war, all together," says Pukhayeva. "We had a sharp reorientation of values: abstract values fell away, and only one value remained: life."

Life had become considerably more difficult. Between acts of war and acts of God, Tskhinval was left without gas, electricity or running water. Breadlines were measured in days. The city filled with women wearing black in mourning for sons and husbands. The suffocating safety of the Stagnation Era acquired a new appeal. "I realize this is bad," nodded Natalya Sanakoyeva, an English instructor at the university, "but I want back into Stagnation because for me it was a good and comfortable place." The South Ossetians wanted their material comforts back and, after two years of shooting alternating with looting, they longed for a civilizing influence.

In a land that had a library for every 600 people, things were often best explained through literary analogies. "Margaret Mitchell is very popular right now," explained Pukhayeva, who moonlighted as an English instructor in the university's history department. "Probably because everything that she writes about is happening here right now. We have our own Scarlett, who can see that the world is collapsing and it needs to be saved, but without further horror."

Scarlett would be the sixty-one-year-old revered rector of the university, who in 1993 agreed to step in to save the land. A muscular man who spoke slowly, wore shirts that were a bit too tight, and looked at the world with the clearest pair of blue eyes this side of a newborn Ossetian baby, Ludvig Chibirov gave off an air of innocence that would be disarming even if he were not the leader of a warring nation.

Chibirov was the first of the new wave of South Ossetian politicians. When, like many nations in the former Eastern Bloc, South Ossetia grew disillusioned with young nationalist democrats and turned back to Communists, the country went once again to the intelligentsia. Only this time, instead of the insurgent intellectuals, the electorate banked on the Soviet intelligentsia, the intellectual establishment: the rectors, department heads and well-placed researchers. Since in Soviet times membership in the establishment required at least nominal Communist Party activity, these were some of the likeliest candidates for resurrecting the party whose absence had made South Ossetian hearts grow so fond. This they did quickly, creating a united front and what Uruzmag Dzhioyev, a thirty-two-year-old mathematics instructor and the land's first minister of foreign affairs, called "a fog of promises." On a platform of a kinder, gentler future with light, heat, running water and food at Soviet prices, seventeen Communist Party members were elected to the South Ossetian Parliament, becoming its majority faction. Among them were three generations of rectors of the university – Chibirov's predecessor Pavel Doguzov, his successor Yuri Gagloyti, who now headed the research institute, and the current rector, Georgy Dzhioyev (no relation to the foreign minister).

"The people who have come now, they carry more experience in the knowledge of human history," Pukhayeva told me, trying to convince me that there was no problem inherent in having theoreticians running a state – as long as they were the right sort of theoreticians. Not only were several of them historians, but Chibirov wrote the history of the pedagogical institute and edited the South Ossetian history textbook used by local schools; Pukhayeva's brother Konstantin Pukhayev, another newly minted politician, authored several of its chapters. "So they will not allow destruction," continued Pukhayeva in the same tone of confidence in which she no doubt used to describe the bright Communist future. "They are not politicians, but they know a lot, they are well read, they know what happens in the world, and for this reason they will lead us in step with the world. I think the optimal option for internal politics is a person who knows the essence of humanity, who understands human psychology, who knows how humanity has acted, be it in the time of the Romans or – well, you know, at other times when states were collapsing like this."

*

They may have known what people did as Rome burnt, but did this mean they knew how to govern? Pukhayeva's faith in the wisdom of the philosopher kings was boundless, tempered neither by the scholars' lack of political expertise nor by the magnitude of the problems the new politicians faced. "I am not a chicken," she told me, stating the obvious. "I have never laid an egg, but I know how it's done. They are not politicians; they did not receive specialized education – but politics as we studied it turned out to be bankrupt," said the woman who held a PhD from the Higher Party School of the Central Committee. "If the person is on the level, if he carries the baggage of knowledge, experience, intellectualism and nobility and patriotism and internationalism – then that is politics, regardless of what your education was."

Some South Ossetian politicians did acknowledge to me that in practice the business of politics required some skills that were new for historians and philosophers. Batradz Kharebov, possibly the least outgoing person in the land, admitted that his work as deputy minister of information "requires certain qualifications, maybe even certain connections, to know what people we should seek contact with, whom we can trust with information, whom we can get information from quickly." The forty-four-year-old PhD in economic history and a former staff member at the research institute still seemed most comfortable communicating in writing or not at all. But, he said, "There was nobody who could do this. I had to train on the job. I have to have contact with a lot of different people. I've had to learn the basics. I had to learn to talk on the phone."

I had some difficulty believing that no one else was willing to do Kharebov's job. During its most recent parliamentary election South Ossetia had distinguished itself from the rest of the world in a new way. With one out of every hundred voters seeking a seat in Parliament, South Ossetia had more aspiring politicians per capita than, possibly, any country in the world. This extraordinary statistic notwithstanding, local office holders demonstrated remarkable unity in claiming to have been dragged into politics kicking and screaming after South Ossetia lost faith in the young nationalist-democrats. The willingness to step into a government job for which one does not appear qualified had, to them, become a mark of outstanding patriotism.

Atsamas Kabisov, a thirty-four-year-old bearded painter who reluctantly served as Chibirov's deputy for defense, maintained that he had no choice about picking up a gun and later accepting a government position. "Somebody had to do it," he argued. "And Rodin once said that an artist must be a citizen first."

Chibirov claimed to have been "literally forced to become chair of the Supreme Soviet," having demurred twice before being elected unanimously (which does mean that he voted for himself). Once Chibirov was elected, civic duty began knocking on the doors of many of his former colleagues. "Chibirov and I have a long-standing relationship: he is a historian, and I am a historian," explained Pukhayev, Chibirov's forty-two-year-old co-author, a PhD in South Ossetian history of the Soviet period and a former employee of the research institute. "So when he was choosing assistants, he set his sights on me. I was stubborn, refused for a long time. I had stayed away from power structures because I had long since determined that research would be my main direction in socially beneficial work. But circumstances were such that someone had to stand up next to Chibirov." Now Pukhayev was responsible for monitoring all of the land's social services.

Pukhayev's office mate was one of South Ossetia's most colorful politicians, deputy rector Kosta Dzugayev, who started in government as Chibirov's press secretary. Though this tall dark and handsome thirty-eight-year-old, who had the disconcerting habit of speaking not merely in complete sentences but in well-rounded speeches, appeared born for politics, he too claimed to have been forced into the field. "By the nature of my convictions," he declaimed, "I am – well, I fear appearing immodest – but I am really a philosopher. I ended up in politics because it could not be any other way. . . . To be here and not participate would have been treason. My many friends and colleagues would not have put up with it."

Security minister Viacheslav Bagayev, a colonel in the Soviet military, was one of the few critics of the governing intelligentsia that I managed to find. He could not find it in his heart to feel sorry for the academics who complained about patriotism interrupting their research. "I, for one, love my job," said the lifelong military man. "I know that if I ran for office, I would not be able to do what I love – so I didn't run." On the same commonsensical note, he added, "A person who wants to build a state, if he hasn't had a chance to become a politician, should at least know something about economics and legislation."

Which the new South Ossetian politicians did not. Of the thirty-five sitting members of Parliament, none was a lawyer and only one was an economist – rather, a professor of economics, the former chairwoman of the university's economics department. In the Soviet Union, law and economics were highly ideologized fields of little prestige that few people chose to pursue; those who did were, perhaps, too intimately acquainted with the political process to fit in with the wave of academic politicians.

But while the scholars may have been political dilettantes, they were pros at politicking. Their admixture of state power and academic intrigue was a lethally backbiting brew. According to Uruzmag Dzhioyev, when non-Communist political activists responded to the re-formation of the Communist Party by organizing their own Party of National Unity, two of its founders who worked at the research institute received reprimands for poor attendance from institute director Gagloyti, who was shortly elected to Parliament from the Communist Party. (Gagloyti dodged my attempts at an interview.) Another outspoken young scholar-politician, Evelina Gagloyeva, was removed as chair of the university's economics department following the first session of Parliament. Proving the tactic effective, Gagloyeva refused to speak to me, passing through a colleague the message that she was "fed up with the whole thing."

Soviet scholarship was strictly a single-truth institution. To chairman Chibirov, that still seemed like the natural order of things. "My line in Parliament is that there is no Communist Party and there are no other parties: there is only the all-Ossetian party, which has to defend the interests of the Ossetian people," he related. "There are individuals within Parliament and outside of it who do not share the main positions of the government, but they do not talk about it openly."

Like political science that was taught in the university, the official line propagated inside the Parliament building blatantly denied the existence of forces other than itself. When, after two days of interviews with Communist Party representatives, I asked communications man Kharebov – whose boss, the minister of information, was general secretary of the Communist Party – to put me in touch with some opposition politicians, he responded with a flat and unselfconscious "We don't have an opposition." Pressed on this point, he grew defensive, told me the opposition had left town, that if I wanted to talk to them I would have to get my information elsewhere, and that the opposition paper *Ard* had shut down. When I insisted on my own truth, he did what any Soviet professor would have done: he shut me out, refusing to talk to me for the rest of the week I spent in South Ossetia.

"He overreacts," sorrowfully noted my polyester-clad companion, whose role now seemed to have switched to tracking rather than guiding me. "Opposition is a painful subject." So painful that in at least one case Kharebov personally called to cancel an interview appointment I had scheduled with someone else. The crudity of his action was almost seductive: training on the job, he was a politician who had not yet learned that information control must be imperceptible to be effective. The subtleties of spin eluded him. When I asked him for clippings on the history of the South Ossetian conflict, he enthusiastically handed me a pile of materials that, on closer examination, proved to be books and scholarly essays on South Ossetian history. For a historian who, by his own admission, had spent his entire adult life bent over a book, politics was simply not a thing of the moment.

As any Soviet scholar knew, the advantage of history over current events – long-ago history especially – was its extraordinary malleability. Contemporary politics, however stately it may have appeared in the speeches of scholar-politicians inside their Parliament offices, had a way of rearing its disheveled head. It peeked through the bullet holes in the curtains of the apartment where I stayed, stared out the barrel of a gun pointed at me by a group of young men cruising Tskhinval in a car in the afternoon, and declared itself in nightly post-curfew gunfire.

"It's very hard to work here," noted the understated Ibragim Arifi, director of the all-volunteer independent television station Ir. "You are judged with a submachine gun." This the new politicians learned quickly.

The academics "think they are very important," said Znaur Gassiyev, first deputy chairman of Parliament who, at seventy, must have been the oldest Communist Party hand in the land (though, being a good South Ossetian, in his youth he did time as a history teacher before going into a career in the Party). "At the first session of Parliament, they all sat down together: Pavel [Doguzov], the former rector, next to the new rector, and they thought that now they were all there and would get to work and everything would be in order. They got burned right away. They even got shot at." One night in April, someone opened fire first on the house of university rector Georgy Dzhioyev and then the house of research institute director Gagloyti.

Then, according to Georgy Dzhioyev, he got an anonymous call saying, "Keep working as rector. We respect you. Teach our children, but leave politics alone." Dzhioyev said that kind of threat can't drive him out of politics, though, as I learned from his colleagues, the rector did attempt to resign his Parliament seat following the shooting. As for Gagloyti, who appeared to avoid me like a new natural disaster, Tskhinvalis in the know said he had stopped going to government meetings.

But whether the shootings reported by the rectors were indeed a trial by fire was the subject of much debate in Tskhinval. Virtually every non-Communist seemed convinced that the shootings were staged to raise the pair's political profiles. Defense minister Bagayev even suggested that the incidents were an attempt to settle an old score – say, by a student who had been made to pay a bribe to enter the university.

Nothing was quite what it seemed in wartime, it seemed. Civil war, Chibirov told me in his authoritative-historian voice, is the scariest kind of war there is, because of the havoc it wreaks on the national psyche. One effect that seemed to have taken the new politicians by surprise was that in this land, where elders had always had the final word and teachers were nearly equated with saints, the younger generation had begun to look at its former teachers with disrespect bordering on disdain. The population of Tskhinval was divided along lines of grave suspicion, and the divisions were rendered in the black and white of polarizing crisis: the young versus the old, those who fought in the war versus those who didn't, and those who are patriotic versus those who are presumed to work for the Georgians. South Ossetian Parliament chairmen were declared traitors to the nation and removed by their colleagues on an annual basis, though their putative acts of treason would fail to impress most observers as in any way extraordinary.

The opposition was now made up almost entirely of young men who fought in the war; they did nothing to disguise their disdain for and lack of trust in the current leadership – or anyone else who had not fought in a war (even though many of them had returned to the university, where they were taught by these very elders). A red-faced and red-bearded military commander with three university degrees (in medicine, geology and engineering) who would allow me to refer to him only as Alexander the Great refused to talk to me unless I proved I could handle a Kalashnikov. After three hours of shooting practice, having concluded that I was an able shot, Alexander felt free to ruminate on the fate of the land. Casting a despairing look over the city from the mountain we used as a shooting range, Alexander said that as long as a single non-warrior remained in government, South Ossetia would likely be sold to Georgia and "a period of terror, civil war and so on" would begin. The dominant conspiracy theory was that a secret deal involving Russia, Georgia and South Ossetia would be cut, and the South Ossetians would be forced to disarm. Why would the South Ossetian politicians cut such an unprofitable deal? Because, the theory went, when Georgians occupied the city in January 1991, they confiscated the archives of the local KGB, which had reported to Georgia, which had in turn reported to Moscow, which meant that anyone in government could be subject to blackmail and was thus a potential traitor.

The leadership's academic lineage provided further fodder for conspiracy theorizing. The educational institutions here reported to the Education Ministry in Georgia, which was accountable to Moscow. The decades-old habit of relying on Moscow and Tbilisi not only to deliver furniture but to dictate the party line in every discipline had, in the eyes of the opposition, made the scholars resistant to the radical-secessionist politics of the soldiers.

The oratorical Dzugayev was convinced that South Ossetia was equipped to bridge the confidence gap. "It was the high education level in our republic that enabled us, in the briefest of periods, to reach civilized norms of oppositional action," he said. "In our harsh conditions, the opposition movement could have transformed and grown to exert influence by force. That we managed to avoid that is a credit to the working potential of the scholars and the intellectuals, because these people ensured firm limits of social movements. With the exception of some regrettable excesses, such as shooting at people's houses – things did not get further than that."

Against the background of city streets that filled with the sounds of shooting every night, Dzugayev's comments rang disingenuous (kind of like when, after telling me that he wrote his dissertation on dialectical materialism, he said, "I want to underscore that it wasn't in an ideologized area of philosophy"). The politics of opposition in South Ossetia looked and sounded explosive. When the Communist-academic faction took over Parliament, a casualty of the transition was Uruzmag Dzhioyev, the young mathematics instructor and separatist radical who had served as South Ossetia's foreign minister for nearly two years. "Uruzmag's non-confirmation elicited a certain reaction among the young people," euphemistically noted Viacheslav Gobozov, a medical student turned Parliament member and television personality, who was one of the few insurgent intellectuals still in office. "The guys went to the session of Parliament, asked to speak, and asked Chibirov how he could explain it." From this point, accounts diverged, but something about the discussion that followed made people describe it as an attempted military coup. It seems "the guys" may have carried arms and acted rather enthusiastic about their ability to use them.

That coup may have failed, but the possibility of "a period of terror, civil war and so on" seemed palpable without any effort on the part of Georgia or Russia. With all the young men armed and the vast majority of them unemployed and otherwise unoccupied, with the society hopelessly mired in internal and external conflict, and with the economy in a shambles, South Ossetians had taken to shooting one another at an alarming rate.

In 1994, over twenty young South Ossetians, including the deputy defense minister and the head of the police special forces, died from gunshot wounds inflicted by other South Ossetians. In the summer of 1993, fifteen people died when the police decided to execute a gang of soldiers turned robbers, spawning rumors that someone somewhere "knew too much." Each death led to a tense stand-off between and among the city's various armed groupings, but in every case, miraculously, tensions died down after a few days.

The genteel Dzugayev – who, being apparently the only younger member of Parliament not carrying a handgun, had the luxury of shedding his suit jacket in the heat – maintained that the South Ossetian leaders, drawing on their experience as teachers, had managed to avert civil war. Chibirov modestly declined credit. His government's concrete efforts so far had indeed been limited to the tactics of university teachers. Chibirov had met with groups of young men – meetings that, according to him, contained "much unpleasantness" – and asked North Ossetian authorities to grant South Ossetian young men non-competitive admission to higher-education institutions there. The point was to get the armed soldier-children off the streets. With the same goal in mind, the South Ossetian university had decided to raise the number of incoming freshmen.

"And what kind of conditions are they going to set – that everyone who is accepted into the university has to surrender his submachine gun?" laughed Bagayev, the doubting security minister. "In that case, we could open two universities and the war would end. The war is not over. It will be over when we are recognized as a country. That's when we'll solve the arms problem."

A country, as any South Ossetian will tell you, has to be recognized as such by the rest of the world. Chibirov's team, elected on promises of peace, was planning to negotiate with the Georgian side. But this effort was in the earliest of stages, with only an "expert committee" formed to assess the prospects of starting the process – which looked none too substantial.

But what else does it take to make a country? Well into their fourth year of struggling under the rubble of a collapsed infrastructure, South Ossetians would also tell you with certainty that a country must have an economy – which, at first glance, South Ossetia appeared to lack. The few factories that existed here stood still and empty, looted largely three years ago by their managers in flight. Most of the land's agriculture was also pre-war history now, since virtually all of the cattle had been killed or stolen. Every house and apartment in Tskhinval had a bathtub filled with cold water from a well; there was no other source of water. After living without light for over two years, Tskhinval residents finally secured electricity by stretching cables out their apartment windows to a giant battery that was wired across the Russian border into North Ossetia. Being unable to tap into the Russian supply of natural gas, South Ossetians continued to rely on Georgia for this – and the Georgian side (which could hardly boast of natural-gas riches itself) seemed to enjoy playing practical jokes. There was no gas throughout the cold winter, but in the spring it was turned on with such force that attempts to light the stove were either futile – the force of the gas blew out the match – or dangerous, if the fire caught. Pensioners and state employees – who included all politicians and academics and those who were both – had not been paid since Chibirov took office in September 1993. In an attempt to stave off mass hunger, the city handed out small plots of land to residents, who planted vegetables, which they tended every day after lunch, when they departed their places of employment *en masse*.

"So we have many problems, of a political, social and economic nature," acknowledged Chibirov vaguely. "As a result of the collapse of the USSR, our country has become impoverished to some extent." From all appearances, the land had been impoverished to the extent of post-war Tara, and the relationship that had to the collapse of the USSR was that aid from Moscow – which had been the focus of South Ossetian foreign policy for the last several years – was drying up.

"What do our leaders do?" Georgy Dzhioyev asked rhetorically. "They go and ask, 'Please give us some money so we can give it out for people to buy bread.'" In other words, they tried to work along the channels to Moscow that had always worked for them, funding and controlling their educational institutions. But, as the laws of economics would have it, the money they got had a way of leaving South Ossetia as soon as it was spent on imported bread. Dzhioyev's solution was to get local industry up and running again. "I suggest this: we get some loans," he enthused. "We have a wonderful climate, we have the woods and natural resources, with roads and everything. So gradually we'll get some small enterprises working. And make them turn a profit fast, so we don't have to always live on credit."

That plan, according to Georgy Dzhioyev, was the result of "many meetings." There were still a few kinks in it, though. First, the dominant Communist Party, of which Georgy Dzhioyev was a member, was not keen on private property. Most South Ossetian politicians, Georgy Dzhioyev included, opposed continued privatization and decried Gorbachev's reforms as the root of all evil: the collapse of the Soviet Union and South Ossetia's current predicament. Chibirov's fear was that "our republic is so insignificant that one wealthy person, if allowed to do so, could buy up all the useful land. And then where would we put the population?" The second obstacle was that the plans for rejuvenating the local economy did not get any more specific than Georgy Dzhioyev's exclamations. The third kink was that the South Ossetian economy had already taken on a life of its own, and it was not of the legal sort.

The former deputy chairman of the South Ossetian Parliament was facing charges of corruption and embezzlement. Reports of a South Ossetian gun-smuggling mafia popped up regularly in the Russian press. Local politicians had the unnerving habit of driving around in expensive cars, which, according to Gobozov and others, was a large part of the reasons for the recent rash of murders: they made sensitive and hungry young men just too envious. I made my way from North to South Ossetia in a Defense Ministry vehicle with an Ossetian peacekeeper, a young businessman, and a member of Parliament who claimed to be the person in charge of finances at the ministry. Our car – a new white Italian-made all-terrain vehicle – made a stop at a North Ossetian bank, where the politician collected an impressive pile of large bills. "Salaries," he explained as he packed the pile into the car. Probably the ones that had not been paid in nine months.

The fourth and final obstacle on the way to a vibrant South Ossetian economy was that, while the most recent crop of South Ossetian politicians knew a lot about history and philosophy, most of them were neither informed about nor particularly interested in economics. "So far the work of Parliament has been limited to shifting around personnel," claimed Uruzmag Dzhioyev. I found little evidence of other activity, save for education reform. In the middle of the week I spent in South Ossetia, most members of Parliament disappeared; their staff explained that they had gone to North Ossetia on government business. Truthful Chibirov told me that that day the capital of North Ossetia was hosting the opening of a conference on Ossetian studies that he – and many of his colleagues in the academy and the Parliament – simply could not miss. In the two months following the last election, the Parliament met only once. "You'd think everything was fine in Athens," Uruzmag Dzhioyev commented caustically. The presidium of Parliament, made up of the ministers and committee heads, met more frequently. But evidence of state-building activity was scarce. On the agenda for the presidium meeting that fell during my stay in South Ossetia were discussion of the South Ossetian state award and a report-back on Znaur Gassiyev's trip to Moscow in search of further financial aid.

When I asked politicians what the Parliament did, they told me about committees. "On every committee, we've got professionals. We, for example, sit on the committee on science, education and culture," said Georgy Dzhioyev, nodding toward former rector Pavel Doguzov and Anatoly Kabarayev, chairman of the university's philosophy department. "There is a committee on economics: that's where the economists sit. Then we have, say, a committee on legislation. That's where lawyers sit. So they just work things out and we approve them."

The problem was, there were no lawyers and only one economist. Dzugayev, who headed the committee on legislation, was openly resentful that he did not get to chair the education committee, where the action was. That committee was working on education reform, the Parliament's favorite child. When they finished, South Ossetian children would have specialized education for the last two years of secondary school, the better to prepare them for college.

"The presidium meets frequently, I think." Doguzov advanced a defense of the government's honor. "So there is work going on. And the voters come often too – our students especially come with questions. Sometimes they stop us in the street: What's going on with the pensions, when are we getting them? I say that we are waiting, we are waiting, and help is going to come from someplace." That was probably as accurate an expression of South Ossetia's economic strategy as there was.

The front page of an issue of the opposition newspaper *Ard* opened with a crude drawing of a young man, armed to the gills, and a skeptical-looking gentleman with a briefcase, separated by a dotted line on the ground. The young soldier's side was marked "South Ossetia"; the gentleman's "The Rest of the World." The caption read: "The World Community: 'Somehow, I don't recognize you, dear.' South Ossetia: 'Maybe that's a good omen and it means I'll be rich.'" The joke referred to a Russian superstition that holds that a person not recognized by an acquaintance will come into money.

Desperate times call for defiant humor. But on the day I met with the publishers of the paper – Alan Kachmazov and Inga Kochiyeva, a young married couple – their mood was far less hopeful than the paper would have suggested. They talked of ever-worsening economic conditions, bitterly listing the latest bloopers of the administration – their former teachers. They pumped me thirstily for news of journalist friends in Moscow. Though they were among the most visible members of the radical-secessionist opposition, they could not hide their desperation in the face of South Ossetia's attempt at statehood. They hinted they might soon abandon the project; indeed, about a year later they moved to Moscow.

On the hill at the end of the street on which Kachmazov and Kochiyeva lived – Soviet Street, known as Death Street during the shelling, because it was targeted from every direction – stood the largest structure in Tskhinval: the unfiinished new building complex that would have housed the university and its dormitories. It was as grand and unfinished a project as the South Ossetian experiment in independence;

what remained of it after the war was a steel carcass filled with darting shadows of young men who now used it as a shooting range.

The old university building, a pink neoclassical structure in the center of town, was now decorated with a wall of photographs of students who were killed in the war. Though it was a source of particular pride around Tskhinval that the university did not close even for a day during the war, students said that the academic learning process ceased when the war began. "You can imagine that after the war, we have nothing left," said the rector, Georgy Dzhioyev. "The equipment is all gone: Everything has been destroyed or stolen. If things settle down and we start off on the right foot, I have more work here, in the university, than there, in Parliament."

All the scholar-politicians professed a burning desire to leave politics and return to academe. Chibirov, who was made rector emeritus when he became chairman, noted with satisfaction, "The university's doors aren't closed to me yet." Dzugayev, Kharebov and Pukhayev all could not wait to resume their research – and to build on their experiment in governing in their study of history and philosophy.

"I have some interesting thoughts on the development of national spiritual and world-view nucleus," explained Dzugayev, the adherent of dialectical materialism. "The Ossetians, in this respect, represent an interesting object of study. The ethical constants that were maintained in our society for centuries are taking on new shapes under new conditions, thus influencing the development of the ethnicity as a whole." Perhaps if he ever wrote about this he might make it comprehensible.

Some of the strongest "ethical constants" in South Ossetian culture were the traditional respect for elders and teachers and the value placed on education. Now that teachers had stepped into an area where unsuccessful experiments were not merely the basis for further study and where faulty theories could contribute to war and destruction, they had, perversely, lost much of their status. Alexander the Great left me with an aphorism and an interpretation whose less-than-flawless logic seemed somehow indigenous to this Caucasian land. "We have a saying," he said slowly, as he slipped the magazine in and out of his Kalashnikov almost imperceptibly. "You can make a policeman out of a person, but you can't make a person out of a policeman. So — better to be a good person than a bad politician." That may be the last and most important of the lessons of South Ossetia.

CHAPTER NINE

THE DISSIDENTS REBORN

There is a very particular sort of spectacle to which Russia has treated its citizens and some of the rest of the world throughout the century. It is the spectacle of an individual being trampled by a mob. In 1958 there was Boris Pasternak, who had the audacity to be awarded the Nobel Prize for Literature and became the victim of a mass-media smear campaign. There were Andrei Sakharov and his wife, Yelena Bonner, in 1973, when a well-organized stream of libelous, often violently worded letters flowed into the press. Another fifteen years later it was Sakharov again, now a deputy of the Supreme Soviet, an old and weak man endlessly attempting to speak to thousands of heckling deputies who invariably drowned him out. In 1995 and 1996 it was Sergei Kovaliov, another older man whose soft-spoken appeals caused avalanches of denunciations and vitriol from the Parliament, the government, the media.

In December 1994, when Russian federal troops entered the breakaway republic of Chechnya, Kovaliov, a former political prisoner, publisher of a human rights newsletter and now a member of Parliament and the head of the Presidential Human Rights Commission, flew to the Chechen capital of Grozny. "When we went there," he told me eighteen months later, speaking of himself and a group of deputies and activists who accompanied him, "it was before the start of real warfare and we were still hoping to prevent escalation. We thought that our presence and our information would make the federal authorities want to retreat. Well, we had hope that it would. A bit of hope, the less the longer it went on. And then, of course, the feeling of helplessness came."

Kovaliov, a biologist, had served a ten-year sentence for collecting and publishing information about human rights violations. Information was probably the only weapon he knew. As the conflict in Chechnya escalated, he collected information furiously, driving from one end of the republic to the other recording what he heard and saw, gathering shells and shards as evidence, flying to Moscow to give press conferences and coming back. He became possibly the best-loved, most respected person in Chechnya. Meanwhile in Moscow a mob readied to attack him. In the spring the lower house of Parliament voted to remove Kovaliov from his post as commissioner. Kovaliov got the news from journalists gathered at an airport in which he landed after a trip to Strasbourg, where he had presented his information on Chechnya to the Council of Europe. The evening of his return television screens flashed his tired face, which had become familiar to the entire country in the preceding couple of months. "Well," he said after getting the news from the Parliament, "I was a dissident in Soviet times, and I'll be a dissident now."

If the intelligentsia in general derived part of its identity from its relationship to the regime, then an oppositional posture was the only thing that both defined and united the dissidents. Kovaliov generally claimed to dislike the term for this very reason. "It's imprecise," he would say. "What was dissidence? I would say first of all that it was not a profound difference of opinion with the regime – it was more impulsive than that. Second, it was not a conscious, thought-through resistance movement that would have stood on some sort of a political platform. It was not political opposition. It was simply a moral incompatibility with what surrounded one."

The writer Andrei Siniavsky, imprisoned in the 1960s and later forced to emigrate, once claimed that his difference of opinion with the Soviet regime had a purely "aesthetic nature." It often seemed that to become a dissident one had to pass a certain threshold, accumulate a critical mass of experience with all that was unhuman, immoral and frightfully counter-intuitive about the Soviet system. Often this meant that those who became dissidents had more than the average person's familiarity with the workings of the regime. Sakharov, one of the developers of the Soviet hydrogen bomb, was for years a frequent guest at Central

Committee meetings; his second wife, Yelena Bonner, who greatly aided him in identifying his causes, was herself the daughter of a Central Committee member killed in the Stalinist purges. Sakharov's membership in the Soviet elite helped ensure that his voice carried great weight in the country and abroad, and, paradoxically, added to his unparalleled moral authority as a critic of the regime.

Of course, not all dissidents saw the regime's most unsavory aspects from the top. Kovaliov, for example, drifted into dissidence after writing what he believed was a fairly innocent letter to the authorities at his graduate school objecting to the supremacy of the teachings of Trofim Lysenko, the Soviet antigeneticist. Whoever they were, the dissidents worked in tandem with the regime. It repressed their words, thereby magnifying their importance; they objected to the repression and the arrests; the regime responded with more of the same. This mechanism of interaction was logical and probably the only possible one; few people wondered what would happen if one day the regime suspended its repressive response – would the dissidents continue to criticize?

Starting in about 1987, the regime attempted to change the relationship in such a way that it would make dissidents obsolete. Glasnost brought their words, albeit with certain limitations, into the media. The state moved to do some of the work dissidents had long been demanding it do such as investigate the crimes of Stalinism. The only condition was that the dissidents stop being dissidents. In 1988, for example, the Central Committee, through threats, negotiations and various legal measures, attempted to stop the formation of Memorial, an organization founded to collect information about the victims of Stalinism; the government claimed such a group was unnecessary because the work would be done by newly formed state agencies. In 1987 and 1988, when the vast majority of political prisoners were released, the state sought to preempt their further activity: they were instructed to sign a statement promising not to engage in "antistate activities."

Probably all the dissidents and their allies, in and out of jail, thought this approach to releasing the prisoners reprehensible. The state was making it clear there would be no apologies, no reviews, no guarantee, finally, that the days of violent repression would not return. Some political inmates refused to sign the paper, forcing the authorities to find another way to release them without acknowledging that they had been held wrongly. Still, some of those who had already been released, including Sakharov and Bonner, who were allowed to return to Moscow from their exile in Gorky, advocated signing the statement as though it were a mere formality. Others, including Larisa Bogoraz, who spent years in internal exile and whose second husband, Anatoly Marchenko, had just died in prison, criticized this position bitterly.

This controversy, one of the first to divide the dissidents, was the beginning of a series of debates, both public and private, through which the dissidents attempted to define their new relationship with the regime. It stands to reason that Sakharov was the leader in shaping the cautious new cooperation. He was not only the moral leader of a large part of what we know as the dissidents – the liberals who prefer to call themselves human rights defenders – but he had maintained a series of unique connections to the Soviet regime. Well into the 1970s, after many colleagues and Sakharov himself came to think of him as a pariah, on a couple of occasions, when he felt the situation warranted extraordinary measures, he managed to finagle access to direct government telephone lines and ring such people as then KGB chief Yury Andropov. When Sakharov was released from his exile in the city of Gorky, it was not a police officer or a prison administrator but General Secretary Mikhail Gorbachev who called to deliver the news.

Certainly after the acclaimed scientist became a dissident all of Sakharov's interactions with the power elite were exceptions to the rule of animosity that at times bordered on violence. Only at extraordinary times did one or the other side attempt to locate a point of contact. Perestroika was an extraordinary time. Sakharov's return to Moscow was followed by a chain of high-level meetings that segued into negotiations with the authorities on a variety of issues, including the Memorial effort. By 1989, as the Soviet Union prepared for its first byzantine rendition of a democratic election, Sakharov was straddling the dividing line between the dissident subculture and the ruling culture – a feat that certainly only a man of his stature and reserve could have pulled off. He was poised to make the step to participation in the work of governing.

About eighty territorial districts and institutions nominated Sakharov as their candidate for the Supreme Soviet. Their geography mapped his path: they included the closed nuclear-research town where he had worked and the Academy of Sciences, of which he was a member. Sakharov decided to run from the Academy, sure all the while that nothing would come of it: either the Academy members' political will would fail and he would lose the nomination at the last minute (and this almost happened), or the government would intervene to prevent his election. Once his election began to seem likely, however, Sakharov began to see it as an opportunity to speak to the country of the many things he felt needed to be widely known.

Yelena Bonner had a visceral revulsion to everything connected with the Soviet government. At first she opposed making a bid for Parliament. "There were 2,000 deputies in the Supreme Soviet," she recalled seven years later. "What the fuck did he need that for?" She smiled the smile of a person who has lived and risked enough to earn the right to ignore the expectations of politesse. "But then I stopped resisting," she added. "That state of euphoria of what was supposedly freedom got me, like it did other people."

What followed was the televised spectacle of one man being trampled by a mob. The Congress of People's Deputies in May 1989 was televised for the first time in Soviet history. The streets of Soviet cities emptied; everyone was watching the Congress. Several times they saw an old man, who looked like a teacher or a grandfather but certainly like no Soviet politician, walk slowly to the podium, stand for a moment, hunched over slightly, and then begin speaking softly. His speech was also as different from the apparatchiks' as could be. He spoke the cultivated Russian of a highly educated man. He drafted his short talks carefully, usually over several days, to convey the substance of his argument without the empty jargon that had always filled Soviet political speeches. No one had heard such simply human speech in government before.

No one heard now, either. As Sakharov spoke – at the Congress and later, at other sessions, on the need for open elections of the chairman of the Supreme Soviet (this post was held by Gorbachev), then on the need to repeal Article 6 of the Constitution, which guaranteed the supremacy of the Communist Party, on the shameful legacy of the war in Afghanistan – the hall would transform. People would rise from their seats, louder and louder and louder clap with every sentence. This was not the applause of encouragement or recognition. This was mean, energetic, loud clapping intended to silence the speaker. Buoyed by the crowd, Gorbachev did his part in silencing Sakharov. A national television audience watched as he addressed Sakharov in the irritated tone in which a school principal might scold a naughty boy. Then he turned off Sakharov's microphone.

The symbolic persona of Andrei Sakharov really consisted of two extraordinary people: Sakharov and Bonner. If Bonner had not reversed her opposition to Sakharov's election, he would surely have refused to run. I asked Bonner if she felt sorry to have given up that fight. "Listen," she said. "Once he was elected, there was little for me to do: sit at the typewriter until four in the morning, drive the car and cook bortsch. And that's all." She smiled. "And all the rest too." In a book of memoirs completed in 1989 Sakharov described their interaction during the Congress: Bonner would watch the proceedings on television, then, as soon as a break was announced, jump behind the wheel and drive to Red Square to meet her husband for lunch, to process and strategize.

Over the next seven months Bonner and Sakharov formulated his position on a number of issues, from the Tiananmen Square massacre in China to Sakharov's support for Gorbachev (which he termed "conditional"). Sakharov had allies in the Supreme Soviet, including the members of the Interregional Deputies Group, which he co-chaired with Boris Yeltsin and Galina Starovoitova and several others, but the majority of the deputies continued to unleash their venom when Sakharov took the stage. Sakharov died on December 14, 1989, leaving much of the country feeling as though it had witnessed his slow murder. A few hours before his death he spoke about the need for radicalizing reform. He left a prepared speech on the flaws of the new Basic Criminal Law.

On December 11, 1989, Sakharov convinced his old ally and friend Sergei Kovaliov to run for the Supreme Soviet of the Russian Federation in the 1990 election. "We met to discuss it," Kovaliov told me, "and I was inclined to refuse to run. I reasoned that he was already a member of the Supreme Soviet of the Soviet Union, so we already had a parliamentary pulpit – and one was enough. It seemed to me it would be better if I worked on other things – and there were things to work on – but he said, 'You simply must run,' so I ended up promising him, and three days later he died and then there was no turning back." Over the years that followed Kovaliov grew into the role of Sakharov's heir. Journalists reporting on his work in Chechnya often remarked on his manner of speech, slow and softly righteous in a way reminiscent of Sakharov.

After Sakharov's death, journalists, writers and others who express their thoughts publicly took to referring to the dead dissident as "our conscience." Kovaliov inherited the thankless job of battling complacency and pragmatism, all the while attempting to define the proper relationship between the intelligentsia – or any other group that would have him as its conscience – and the state. "The idea that perhaps something that was coming from above, from the regime, deserved some sort of limited, conditional support occurred to me as far back as 1988, maybe even in late 1987," Kovaliov remembered. "Sakharov and I discussed this when he decided to participate in that election and many dissidents opposed it. And my agreement to run in 1990 was also a sort of decision to attempt to cooperate with the regime and to attempt to exert a more direct influence on government decisions. I understood that this sort of cooperation would be, at the least, very difficult. But I should say that the level of difficulty exceeded my expectations – a long time ago, long before I came into direct conflict with the top authorities."

Of course, from the moment Kovaliov took his first steps toward a new relationship with the authorities, he existed in indirect conflict with them. Virtually all of his work was aimed at a single goal: limiting the power of the regime. It is telling that for his first attempt at cooperation with the state Kovaliov organized a group to draft a new law on the state of emergency. They were moved in part by the ethnic conflicts that were clearly brewing in various parts of the Soviet Union – and in part by the lack of guarantees that state terror would not return again, as it did after the Thaw. "You see, a state of emergency is a very convenient occasion for instituting an authoritarian regime, or totalitarian, or any regime," Kovaliov explained. "You wake up in the morning and there are tanks in the street. And then what are you going to do? So law on the state of emergency is extremely important for individual rights because it introduces limits to the power of the regime and makes it accountable to the Parliament, and limits what can be done and for how long and through what procedure. So that the state of emergency does not become permanent."

So a group of former inmates and their friends, schooled as biologists, physicists, mathematicians, sat down to educate themselves about legislation writing, international standards, foreign precedent, and to draft the law – all this on an emergency basis, because a bill on the state of emergency was to be presented to the Supreme Soviet of the USSR on November 1, 1989. They brought their bill to the Interregional Deputies Group, which found it too daring but promised to use it as a basis for amendments. The Soviet Union expired before it got a law on the state of emergency; but the dissidents' bill became law in the Russian Federation.

In January 1995, almost exactly five years after Kovaliov and his allies finished working on their bill on the state of emergency, a possible state of emergency was all Kovaliov and his allies could talk about. At the hotel to which Kovaliov and members of his group returned every evening after collecting evidence and testimony around Chechnya, someone would invariably start spinning a macabre fantasy about the introduction of the state of emergency. The scenario was usually roughly the same: the war in Chechnya would enable Yeltsin to declare a state of emergency there, then he would gradually expand it to other parts of the country, giving authorities absolute power, canceling elections and democracy itself for the foreseeable future.

President Yeltsin never did introduce a state of emergency – probably because of the legislation written by Kovaliov and his group. The law was written in such a way that a state of emergency would have prevented the deployment of the federal army in Chechnya; it required that Parliament not only sanction the measures taken but remain in session as long as the state of emergency was in effect so that the situation could be monitored – in other words, said Kovaliov, "there would have been no way to conduct that war." Of course, the government found a way to conduct the war, and to do this it had not needed to conjure clever legal schemes to circumvent the law – it simply ignored it. For most of the century, the governments of Russia and the Soviet Union had ignored many different laws, some of them inspired and fair, others simply inconvenient. The laws had changed, as had the people writing them; but the ways of the state had not.

Kovaliov claimed he had understood this much, much earlier, when he first entered the Supreme Soviet. "There was a traditional system of governing," he said. "The demands of a new time appeared to change the system of government. But there was no other model. So the recreation of the old system began, and has now been completed. The old system has one word that defines it: *nomenklatura*. The *nomenklatura* system of hiring, the *nomenklatura* structure of the administration, *nomenklatura* ways of decision-making." In the Supreme Soviet this meant that virtually all resources were centered in the hands of the Speaker. He had the staff, the information and the power to set the agenda and steer the enormous ship. The elected deputies – most of whom knew little about government, law, the economy or other issues at hand, and, having no support staff, had little chance to learn or even to keep up with the flow of information – became, as Kovaliov put it, "symbolic, I would even say *ritual* figures."

Kovaliov was perhaps luckier than most of the disoriented deputies because he had a clear goal. Ultimately he wanted to create the post of an official ombudsman, a person who, aided by sufficient financial and human resources, would monitor the government's record on human rights. He moved steadily toward this goal. President Yeltsin created a human rights commission, appointing Kovaliov its chairman; a bill creating the post as an independent but state-funded entity was pending in Parliament. Then the war in Chechnya began, the machine that Kovaliov had assembled sprang into action, and the state recoiled at the sight of the monster it had allowed to be created, and immediately moved to disable it. The Parliament attempted to fire Kovaliov (it turned out it did not really have the legal power, since the human rights commissioner served at the pleasure of the President); the President threatened to disband the commission; the defense minister, in classic Stalinese, called Kovaliov "an enemy of the people."

One member of the human rights commission, Yelena Bonner, resigned as soon as the war began. Kovaliov made several statements indicating that the time for cooperating with the regime had passed but plodded along for another thirteen months, hoping that his standing as commissioner would aid him despite official attacks. I asked him what he was feeling over those months about his position. "What could I have been feeling?" he asked in return. "Doubts. Misgivings. Torment. Reversing my decision over and over." Finally, in January 1996, after federal troops demolished the village of Pervomaysky, where a hundred people were held hostage by Chechen resisters, Kovaliov decided he could not continue to be affiliated with the regime.

"Institutions that are even a bit useful – not necessarily effective but at all useful – can be created only by a regime that in some measure seeks to limit its power," he said of the fate of his ombudsman project. "It has to be a regime that is wise enough to understand that this is necessary for the country and for the regime itself. This regime is not going to do any of this. I even have this growing suspicion that no regime, left to its own devices, can do it. It can only arrive at it as a result of pressure – pressure on the part of society. But in Russia we have no civic society, so this pressure is not being exerted."

In other words, he said, "all our efforts came to a big fat nothing." Now it was time to turn away from the government and attempt to build that civic society that might one day transform its government. How would he do that? Kovaliov shrugged: the answer was at once unknowable and obvious. "Speaking. Writing. Starting organizations."

That, in Bonner's none too humble opinion, was the proper work of the intelligentsia. "The intelligentsia is not defined by its education level," she said impatiently. "It is defined by its way of relating to the world, which must be based not on common impressions but only ever on one's own. A member of the intelligentsia is always an individualist. The intelligentsia must always be in opposition to the regime, even if it is democratic – if only because in the absence of opposition any regime becomes inhumane."

I asked if she had not, along with many former and current allies, lived through a love affair with the regime. I remembered seeing her at a Yeltsin support rally in April 1993, standing on the stage next to the President. She shot back, "Listen, I spoke before he arrived. And when he got there and started blathering, I ripped the microphone out of his hands and said, 'Listen, you just have to say: Are you *our* president or not?'" I did not remember her saying this, but then I had stood far away from the stage. In any case, what mattered is that this was how she remembered herself. "Because what is dissidence?" she continued. "It is a way of being in the world. If I lived in Asia or in Europe I would still be a dissident – only the issues would be different."

It seemed like an ungratifying affair the second time around, after a decade when the power structures sucked in so much of the intelligentsia and wrung it out. "I am far more content than those who run scared of the Communists or piss for joy when they see General Lebed entering the government," she responded, and offered to tell me a story. In 1973, when she and Sakharov were being raked over the coals by the mass media, they ran into an acquaintance, a prominent member of the Academy of Sciences.

"How are you?" he asked.

"Fine," they responded.

"Me, I can't sleep," he volunteered. "All because of this witch hunt against you."

"And we are sleeping very well," said Bonner and Sakharov.

Bonner smiled triumphantly at the clarity of her fable. I remembered reading, with some surprise, what Sakharov had written upon the death of Anatoly Marchenko, a man who had spent most of his adult life in the camps as a political prisoner and died in prison at the age of forty-four. Sakharov called Marchenko's life "brief and happy." As a man whose path to his moral position stretched over decades, he must have felt kinship and an almost jealous admiration for one who so clearly lived the strength of his convictions. But in these ever more ambiguous times, did Bonner not feel like the lone island of dissidence in a sea of cooperation?

"I have just as many allies as before," she snapped. "No more and no less. And they are all the same people. With the exceptions of those few who were forced to leave the country." By my count, a great many of Bonner's friends, including her husband, had died; many, including her children, had left the country; and a few had formed a firm association with the Yeltsin regime. Of course, that was the usual predicament for an intelligentsia member, especially one who was seventy-three and Jewish. What made Bonner different was that the certainty she had in her place in society left no room for feeling lonely or unappreciated.

PART FOUR

THE FUTURE

Every generation of the intelligentsia has declared the intelligentsia dead. At other times, it has declared itself the last generation of the intelligentsia. By the usual chronology, the heroes in this part of the book — those who are around or under thirty — are too young to concern themselves with their place in relationship to this great tradition. By the same token, however, they are the people who, in another decade or two, will be calling themselves the last of the intelligentsia. Unless, of course, the intelligentsia is dead.

CHAPTER TEN

GENERATION X, RUSSIAN-STYLE

We live small lives on the periphery; we are marginalized and there's a great deal in which we choose not to participate . . . .

There was . . . too much history there for me. . . . I needed less in life. Less past.

— Douglas Coupland, *Generation X: Tales for an Accelerated Culture*

In the space of three weeks I somehow managed to burn the following objects, all dear to my heart and my purse: the power source of my brand-new inkjet printer, the power source for my Macintosh, another (borrowed) power source for the printer, and two coffee grinders. My apartment filled with the quintessentially electrical olfactory mixture of red-hot metal and melted plastic. I began to suspect I possessed a strange magnetism. Lending credence to this theory, my digital watch with an alarm and two time zones also stopped working.

Something told me I should talk to Natasha, a graduate of the prestigious MIFI, the home of the technological elite. Natasha studied to be a systems engineer, though, like virtually everyone I knew in my generation – those born in the mid- and late sixties – she had never worked a day in her field of expertise. So it was not her education, exactly; it was just that my instincts, sharpened by despair, told me she would somehow be able to help where no single repair shop could be of use.

A few days later Natasha arrived at my apartment accompanied by Igor, a sullen young man who, as it turned out, was another unemployed MIFI graduate. Wasting no time on small-talk formalities, he initiated surgical intervention into the fate of my precious technology. Natasha and I retired to the kitchen, but just a few minutes later we were summoned back by the sweet sound of an advancing sheet of paper and the gurgle of ink squirting. As usual in such informal business arrangements, I felt a bit lost: with private initiative still only partially redeemed, people were saddled with a residual discomfort regarding all monetary transactions.

"How much should I pay him?" I asked Natasha in a hurried whisper.

"Are you crazy?" Natasha would have been shouting if she had not been whispering. "He just does this."

My intuition – the same intuition, perhaps, that I had to thank for bringing Igor to my house – told me that Igor had not provided the service "just" like that: it was just the way Natasha and Igor's loose community of overeducated underemployed young people did things. Theirs was a barter economy, a separate moneyless universe of spontaneously organized exchanges of goods, services and opportunities. I figured Igor would resurface in my vicinity, as soon as he figured out how to make use of my acquaintance.

Igor made a repeat appearance a month or two later; in a departure from his usual sullen self, he spoke breathlessly of his new project: he had secured some storage room in a palace of culture that once belonged to the Interior Directorate, where he installed a half-dozen video recorders linked to a laser disc player, all of which would allow him to make pirate videocassette copies of new film discs issued in the United States. He needed a person in the States, and that was what he wanted from me.

I organized the person in the States, but it all ended at that. I caught glimpses of Igor on the horizon a couple of times more before he disappeared altogether. Natasha told me Igor had lost his one-room apartment in some dispute over money (it was in one of those forsaken parts of Moscow where you can distinctly see that the huge city does have borders, because right there the city ended and the forest began). It seemed he owed money or was owed money, which he went to another city to procure, and ultimately he left Moscow or, at least, his old circle.

The story was typical. People of Igor's circle – indeed, people of Igor's generation – were always nursing some project or another, some ingenious scheme that promised much – that, most important, promised the place in society that they had lost the year they graduated college. They had traded that place for their diploma, which marked their exit from the last formal institution with which they would be affiliated. Now that they were in social free-fall, their projects had a way of never materializing.

Russian sociologists who studied the ways people adapt to life in the transitional period advanced the term "value-driven rational thinking," meaning a world view rooted not so much in the imperative of adapting to current conditions as in idealistic beliefs. A 1993 study by the Institute of Social and Economic Problems of the Population claimed that, contrary to the stereotype of this generation as the quickest to adjust, almost a third of all people with this sort of thinking fell between the ages of twenty-one and thirty. The majority of those who said they do not waste time pondering spiritual or eternal values were over thirty; younger people made up only 13 percent of this group.

Members of this generation acted rationally to the extent that they continuously generated projects ostensibly designed to aid their survival. But they based their plans on a magical view of the world as it should be or could be, and though these plans generally came to nothing, these young people never seemed to lose hope. This was not because they were the first generation weaned on market-economy enthusiasm but because they were the true children of the Stagnation Era; they grew up with an unshakeable faith in the permanence of everyone and everything. Unlike their parents and siblings – older or younger – they lived through their childhood and adolescence without having to cope, even from a distance, with a compelling historic event. They entered young adulthood with a firm belief in the future, a future not so great as it was gray, since its image was indistinguishable from the present.

I had to climb a stairway of the sort that one finds only in St Petersburg: dark, crumbling under my feet, and yet undeniably grand. Every door frame was covered in a cobweb of wires leading to uncountable doorbells: one for each resident of the communal apartments, which suggested both that the flats were huge and that relations within them were chilly (friendly neighbors tend to have just one bell). Yulia's door had a half-dozen bells. She had a total of eleven neighbors, which, statistically speaking, was par for the course: this generation had the lowest percentage of people living in their own flats and the highest percentage of residents of communal apartments. Yulia wasted no time in informing me that her neighbors were not, unlike most neighbors, alcoholic but were nonetheless sadistic and that three years earlier she and her small son had moved into a squatter settlement to escape them, and that there her little boy became infected with tuberculosis.

Mutual acquaintances who arranged my meeting with Yulia had clearly warned that I was interested in the measure of her maladjustment to post-Soviet conditions, so she was forthcoming with her son's tragic medical history, as well as with the announcement that she had no food of any sort and no sugar to go with tea. We drank bitter black tea on the sunny side of the wardrobe that divided Yulia's room in two, and she told me the story of her life: a privileged childhood as a professor's daughter, books and books, a concomitant reluctance to mature, an earnestly literary wish to be just like the Decembrists' self-sacrificing wives and, finally, a dream: "I had this ideal that I would spend my entire life working at the Peter-Paul Fortress," Yulia recalled, referring to a notorious old prison that had been turned into a museum. "I worked in the manuscript department there, and I liked it, and when a person likes something, she thinks that it will last a lifetime."

Yulia cried at the death of Brezhnev in 1982. "I thought that everything was collapsing and there would be a war because our country was careening into instability," she offered by way of explanation for such a display of emotion at the end of what was arguably the least emotional period in Russian history. "Before perestroika, everything seemed stable to me. I had a clear vision: I would attend the university, at twenty-two I would marry, and by the time I was thirty I would have two children and I would speak at the twenty-ninth Party congress." Fifteen years in advance of the planned congress, Yulia wrote the text of her planned speech, which, alas, she did not preserve for posterity.

Yulia graduated the history department of Leningrad State University in 1989. Like many in her generation, who tended to have children early, she gave birth during her fourth year in college. She was not assigned to a post at the Peter-Paul Fortress, so she tried out different jobs. She worked at an archive, taught school, and never gave much thought to the question of whether she would make enough to support herself and the baby: at the time a minimal level of well-being was guaranteed virtually everyone. At one point, she was selling pro-democracy newspapers in the street – an occupation both profitable and satisfying until she grew disappointed with all things political. At around the same time, she suddenly realized that her degree in history was no longer a guarantee of a reasonable income – or any income at all – and decided to learn computer-based layout. On a squat table on our side of the wardrobe sat a computer that looked more like a small heap of scrap electronics parts – or like something that might have been put together by Igor or one of his friends. "Don't you mind that it's so scary-looking," chirped Yulia. "It's just that the monitor is made from an old television." It looked more like it was made from an old refrigerator. "In reality, it's a 486." The "scary-looking" monitor displayed an unstable picture of an unfinished game of electronic solitaire.

Computer layout proved to be a source of income, but an unreliable one: new private companies would commission a book or two and then buy computer systems of their own, rendering Yulia's services unnecessary. It is possible, too, that working relationships collapsed because of Yulia's propensity for overstepping the boundaries of a layout artist's role to become a critic. She showed me a brilliantly written six-page "open letter" that convicted the authors of a cultural-studies textbook, which she had been hired to lay out, of incompetence and illiteracy.

As a chaser to the letter, Yulia shoved at me a hefty – eleven typed single-spaced pages – description of her project of a "women's bibliography institute." The text conjured a vague, though meticulously rendered, image of a clearing house for all information pertaining to women or feminism. Her observations of the successes and failures among her acquaintances had convinced Yulia that "you need to create a job for yourself," since all the existing jobs were occupied by people of an older generation. She created this project so that it would be far superior to the Library of Congress, and now she planned to get Western funding for it.

Statistically speaking, Yulia was typical of her generation. One out of three unemployed people in Russia was between the ages of sixteen and thirty (these statistics are based on the numbers of people registered with the Labor Exchange; in reality the percentage of young people among the unemployed may have been even higher). Nearly half of all recent college graduates were unemployed. Between 1990 and 1993, the percentage of college graduates who were able to find a job in their field dropped from 55 to 37. The percentage of college students who expected a job in their field after their studies had been declining steadily, while the proportion of those who had no intention of working in their field grew. Meanwhile, the average age of staff at colleges and universities, research institutes and other employers of educated people steadily increased.

Conventional wisdom in Russia had it that changes in society were to blame for the difficulties of young people. In fact, though, as a demographic entity, the young people of Russia bore a striking resemblance to their Western counterparts – except that the particulars were vastly exaggerated, as are the particulars of virtually any phenomenon shared between Russia and the West. The young people were similar first of all in that they were few. Their parents belonged to the smallest generation in Soviet history, those born during and soon after World War II.

The generation between these "children of war" and their Generation X offspring was the most numerous, exceeding the twenty-two to thirty-two set by a factor of almost two. They were born between 1950 and 1960 – during the baby boom common to all countries affected by World War II. (The immediate post-war years in Russia were a period of grave hardship, so the baby boom began a bit later here than in the West.) In all these countries, the baby boom generation was not only the most numerous but the most successful, saddling the following generation with the expectation of relative failure.

Spiritually, in spite of the apparent singularity of the difficulties

encountered by Russian young people, they bore a striking resemblance
to their Western peers – or at least to that subset of them that Canadian
author Douglas Coupland described in his novel *Generation X*, whose title
sociologists and journalists appropriated to describe the post-boom
bunch. The Gen X concept is that for a variety of reasons members of
this generation are united only by their absence of definition – hence the
X. According to Western pop sociologists, what Gen Xs lack are
formative historic events, some compelling drama to unify them. The
protagonists of Coupland's seminal book are three young people who
have literally fled civilization to live in the desert, where they hold down
"McJobs" – the employment equivalent of McDonald's, or the lowest-
common-denominator way of supporting oneself.

The Moscow Engineering and Physics Institute always had a hell of a job-
assignment system. The luckiest and most talented students with the best
parentage would go to the Kurchatov Institute. The less fortunate would
be shipped off to closed cities that were not marked on any map. MIFI
students were granted security clearances when they entered the school,
giving up much of their freedom of movement in exchange for secure and
interesting work. But when job-assignment time came in 1992, the
number of available postings for the computer-science department was:
one. Then came the announcement that if seniors wanted their diplomas,
they had to sign a request for an independent job search, thereby releasing
the school from its legal obligation to provide a job assignment. My friend
Natasha – the one who brought me Igor – had had no reservations about
signing – and three years later, she still did not. "I want to say a very big
thanks for the 'independent job search,'" she dictated to me, as though
she were addressing her alma mater in her last will and testament. "Thank
you for freeing me of the looming Cheliabinsk 70 and magnetic time cards
and wearing holes in my pants by sitting."

But when she got her degree, Natasha, who had left a small provincial
town to come to college in Moscow, learned that she would have to give
up her residence registration in the school dormitory. Residence registration, the linchpin of the system of population control since the 1930s,

continued to rule and ruin lives in Russia through all the political, legal and social turmoil. Every citizen's internal passport contained a stamp with her legal address. To obtain residence registration in a "desirable" town like Moscow a person had not only to procure a permanent residence – say, buy an apartment or a room at sky-high prices – but pay a hefty sum of money to the city on top of that. In Moscow, whose residence-registration regime was among the most stringent in the nation, a person not registered in the city did not have the right to live there, work there, or get health care there. Even emergency rooms served only those who lived in the corresponding neighborhoods, creating a macabre situation when doctors would tell patients with broken limbs and knife wounds to seek care nearer their homes, which might be hours away.

It goes without saying that people were allowed to vote only where they were registered, meaning that the uncountable young people who lived in cities where they were not registered had also lost their right to vote. Not that most of them cared. There was precious little statistical data on voter participation in Russia, but what did exist showed young people to be the country's most apathetic constituency. None of the young people I knew went to the polls in 1993, though during the previous national elections, in 1991, they not only voted but took active part in the pre-election political process, whether by distributing "pro-democracy" literature or by being active in student political clubs. All declared that it was the August 1991 failed coup that signaled the end of what one of them called "our heroic struggle for democracy." In the months and years that followed the coup, as the nation grew to see the 1991 events as the public tip of a political iceberg, the Gen Xs felt like their bodies on the barricades of democracy had merely served as props in someone else's grand and obscure production.

To Natasha's mind, her lack of basic civil rights and elementary material well-being was not a misfortune but an attribute of unparalleled liberty. "How do I live? Very well." She gave a qualitative answer to my very brass-tacks question. "Often I get help from friends, acquaintances, loved ones. You see, the way I live, I don't necessarily have money at any given time. But if I have money and I am walking down the street, I can just go and spend it.

"Where do I live? That depends. I don't have a home as such. I like it that way. It doesn't bother me."

One of Natasha's "homes not as such" was a room in a two-room communal apartment in a five-story Khrushchev-era slum. The fold-out couch, the fold-out portable cot, and the floors in the room and the kitchen fit up to eight people at a time. The more or less permanent residents were four: Natasha, who in the summer of 1995 was twenty-six; her one-time lover Maria, twenty-four, a singer who sang nowhere; Liudochka, a thirty-three-year-old demure actress who acted nowhere; and Tania, a twenty-nine-year-old producer who actually had a job with a prestigious movie studio but got paid sporadically, if at all. It was not acceptable to come to this home without bringing food. Fortunately, visitors were frequent – daily, really – and numerous, because this place was comfortable and, more important, interesting. One could always leaf through the latest poetry books, usually procured through mysterious extramonetary means; one could always get an update on the capital's theater, film or music scene. When it came to culture, this was definitely a consumerist, if moneyless, household.

"If Liudochka says to me, 'Let's go to the theater,' I know that means that she got a call from an old classmate who said, 'We have a première today. Why don't you come?'" Natasha was taking pains to explain the system to me. "So why then would I buy a ticket if Liudochka is waiting for me by the stage door?"

A central lesson of the Russian Generation X was that everything that could be done for money could also be done for free. All one needed was time – an unlimited amount of free time. As this last generation to receive a Marxist-Leninist education was taught, time is the market contribution of a person who has nothing.

Twenty-five-year-old Olga arranged to meet me at a fashionable Moscow café called *Krizis zhanra* – The Crisis of Genre – where the clientele was mostly New Russians and young foreigners. Olga, who graduated Moscow's prestigious Literary Institute in 1994 with a degree in literary criticism ("a profession that has been eliminated for lack of demand," she told me in a masterfully wry tone), was neither a New Russian nor a well-off foreigner, though she barely hesitated to tell me that she was largely dependent on both.

"You've got to have talent to not work," Olga – full-bodied and blue-eyed – informed me. "You have to know how to occupy yourself. That's not so simple."

Olga defined her talents as follows: "I finagle money using the means of our democratic era. Sometimes, like when I invested in the MMM [giant pyramid scheme], it doesn't work. Other times – I have certain assets: sexual, physical, intellectual. It helps me to know good people – because in Russia there have always been and still are a lot of good people." "Good people" who were male provided many of the necessities in Olga's life: the basement room in quiet central Moscow, which Olga shared with a friend, was equipped with a contemporary music system, a cordless telephone, and an excellent television with a video player. The last was particularly useful because "screenings" of pirated tapes always drew at least a few friends, who knew to bring food.

(Though all that was strictly temporary. Olga planned to attend the Foreign Trade Academy, whatever that was. She had already earned a second degree at the Russian-American Business College, but that venture proved fruitless. She was sure she would be luckier in her next stab at attaining marketability.)

Olga grew up in the Siberian city of Krasnoyarsk. Like Natasha, she came to Moscow to go to college, and, also like Natasha and like an untold number of young people, she now lived without residence registration or any of the pursuant rights. She claimed to be happy with her living conditions "because I am lucky not to be spending my nights at the railroad station." She pointed out the landmarks of her residence: a toilet with a missing water tank and a rig of a tin basin held in place with a brick for a purpose I could not discern; books and bed mattresses nearly destroyed by the mice that kept the women up at night. While Olga' roommate, Sveta, was a close friend, their flatmate was an enemy for life. Olga and Sveta had to put up with regular middle-of-the-night visits by the district policeman, who knew that the young women, who had no rights in this city, would not dare deny hospitality. "We have to sacrifice in certain respects," Olga admitted. "Like certain living comforts." But, she implied, nothing else.

Natasha clarified it for me. "You can do anything without money," she said. "Starting with going to the theater and up to riding around Moscow at any time of day or night or going south at the height of the season."

There was something mindboggling about this. Statistics showed that the number of Russians who had the time and money to travel for their holidays – a tradition until just a few years earlier – had dropped drastically: more than a third of all Muscovites stayed home in the summer of 1995, and only 1 percent went south. But among the Gen X representatives I interviewed, all but one traveled south to the Black Sea that summer (not even counting those whose interviews fell through because the potential subjects departed for resorts south). The reason here was not just the near-fanatical Gen X devotion to the value system of the Stagnation Era, but, more generally, their relationship to time. Like the heroes of Coupland's book, who escaped to the desert to find the time and space to walk with dogs and admire cacti, the Russian Xs were refugees from an accelerated culture. Like them, of course, but more so.

Tania, an artist educated as an architect, who quit her job with great relief a month after she graduated the Moscow Engineering and Building College in 1990, maintained that what united the inhabitants of the moneyless space was their ability to manage their time "like before." Those who had entered and stayed in the rat-race had time neither for the Crimea nor for the cinema. Whereas Tania continued to travel as she always had: when she felt like it, wherever she felt drawn, to spend exactly as long as felt right. Two years earlier she spent six months in Novosibirsk; the year before she went off to Germany to oversee a spontaneously organized one-person exhibit and stayed on for three months; the summer of 1995 I caught up with her – a Muscovite – in St Petersburg: it was White Nights season, after all.

Poverty had hit suddenly about four years earlier. Like many other young artists, she had been selling her work on the Arbat, a pedestrian mall in the center of Moscow that was, seemingly overnight, overrun with vendors of gaudy souvenirs: wooden Matrioshka dolls, black lacquer boxes and mass-produced decorative watercolors. Tania, like other artists who inhabited the Arbat, was unprepared to be forced out: as befits Gen X, she had held an unshakeable faith in the Arbat's immortality as a hangout and as a source of income. Now she was forced to regress, re-experience life marked by lack of money and financial dependence on her mother. Still, unlike some of her peers, she decided not to take a job as a sales clerk in one of Moscow's countless kiosks, which sold everything from cigarettes and beer to bananas and underwear and whose owners had no regard for residence registration or other formalities. "It's not like the love of art kept me out of the kiosks." Tania wanted to make this perfectly clear. "Nothing can stop me from being an artist. It's that I am unwilling to sacrifice my temporal freedom."

As she adjusted to her new status, Tania made a discovery: "Your standard of living doesn't change. It's time that changes. When you have money, you have no time. Your needs change. Where I used to take taxis to get to work or meetings on time, now I go up to the ticket checker in the Metro and say, 'Miss, please let me through without a token' – and I am not ashamed, because I really don't have any money. On the other hand, the theater, the cinema and other hangout places are accessible without money. Which I take advantage of."

The Russian Gen X was hyperaware of the need for sacrifices. They abhorred the obliviousness with which others forfeited time and immediate freedom. In a world of pointless sacrifices, the Gen Xs hoarded their meager assets. Nest-building Gen X style was an introverted, even asocial process: while New Russians drove their Porsches and Jeeps at breakneck speed on highways outside Moscow, rushing to their new red-brick dachas – still under construction, still empty inside – Gen X's went about the slow and satisfying process of setting up tiny snatches of space they had wrestled away from time, turning them into shrines to their untimely values. Coupland's heroes inhabit desert bungalows where "everything is perfect." Russian Xs constructed their oases of uncommonly comprehensive libraries or surround-sound music systems in horrific communal apartments.

Behind a door with twelve bells, I found a giant hall, large enough to be converted into a comfortable apartment for a small family or, perhaps, a modest little casino. The casino idea struck me when I saw Sergei, who came out to greet me wearing a New-York-style ersatz 1920s get-up; to be precise, it put me in mind of the Cotton Club, which, I think, was the design. As it turned out, Sergei was shooting a movie about the art nouveau aesthetic. He had been shooting it for a long time – or, rather, it had been several years since he started looking for a sponsor for his film, having storyboarded his dream creation in painstaking detail. It looked like he had come to live the aesthetic. The room he shared with his wife, Marina, epitomized the oasis of perfection for which Gen X strove; it was their miniature world, made all the more attractive by its lack of connection to the country or the decade. Everything there – from an antique Turkish coffee pot with a bent matching spoon to a tray with a pair of wire-rimmed glasses placed in it pseudo-casually – fit with the 1920s Chicago-gangster aesthetic. There was nothing superfluous or incidental. Even the water stains on the wallpaper over the double bed seemed like an integral part of the design. Over the course of one and a half hours that I spent in this room, I attempted to ascertain where they had hidden the wardrobe (under the bed, perhaps?); some bulky Russian dark-wood armoire would not have fit with the image of Sergei and his domicile any better than did the object of my inquiry: the young couple's moneyless existence. Sergei refused to speak with me and attempted to stop his out-of-this-place (like the décor) beautiful wife from speaking.

"Don't you understand that this is bad for my image?" he demanded of her. "If you wanted to talk about drug use or my homosexual past, then I would be happy to give an interview, because that's good for my image. But when you are talking about how we don't have any money or anything to eat, then forget it, because that can only be bad for my image."

"So why don't you talk about how you have no money to buy grass?"

suggested a mutual friend who had brought me to their home and was now desperate to cut the tension.

Oh, no. Now Marina and Sergei stared at us in shock that just might have been horror. They could not imagine not having grass. They could imagine – easily – not having food: "You can do without, you can go to someone's house, you can wait until someone comes to see you and brings cookies," Marina explained to me patiently. She was no longer playing up their image; now she was sincerely explaining their value system to me. Grass was not a luxury like a taxi, or an episodic necessity like food. Grass was a way of perceiving reality, a filter that could become a daily, non-negotiable necessity for those whose lives proceeded in a different dimension from the rest of the post-Soviet world. Grass was not vodka, which let you forget; grass simply forced time to slow down, perhaps even stop at a moment of perfection, like one of the frames in the aesthetic film of Sergei's plans.

On the whole, this pair's biographies meshed with those of other Generation Xs. Sergei was twenty-six, a doctor's son from the provinces; he came to Petersburg to study something properly technical but quit his studies soon enough, realizing the pointlessness of the pursuit. Marina, twenty-eight, had just graduated the Mukhin Arts School, department of ceramics, which used to have twenty-eight applicants for every slot when Marina started her studies, whereas now there were only a couple of candidates per space (this, too, was no statistical aberration: since the beginning of perestroika, the number of people who wanted to receive higher education – even in such areas as business and accounting – had dropped by nearly half, and art school graduates had the hardest time on the job market). Friends had warned Marina she would feel depressed after graduation, but she was unprepared for the rapid onset of an awareness that "no one needs my degree." The worst part was, "it's the small things that hold you back – like you have to go to the china plant but you don't have a Metro token."

She was not, however, complaining – merely stating the facts. Indeed, she pointed out that the new way of doing things was better because it ensured the survival of the fittest. Her peers in general were not given to complaining – and why should they complain when they always believed in the success of whatever new project? Marina too had some plans for the future – not the distant future, like before ("before, my entire life was strictly planned – Plan A, Plan B – and that's not right; now I just try to get the most accomplished in the smallest amount of time"), but for the most foreseeable future. For example, in a free advertising handout – the only sort of newspaper this group of people seemed to read – she found an ad for a private company selling artwork to decorating New Russians.

"Chill out," admonished our mutual friend, an art promoter. "Sashka has already gone over there. It's ridiculous. They are amateurs."

Marina frowned. A moment later she aired her other plan: going south for a holiday, "and then we'll see." What about money for the trip? "Er, we are trying to make that right now. But we'll go."

This was a joke I heard.

A young American is interviewed about his finances. "I make about $3,000 a month," he says. "My rent, food and other living expenses eat up about 2,500. So theoretically I should have 500 left over at the end of the month. But I don't know where it goes – it just disappears."

A young German answers the same questions. "I make about 4,000 marks a month. My expenses are 3,500. So I should have 500 left over, but I don't know where it goes – it just disappears."

A young Russian is also interviewed. "I have a salary of $50 a month. My expenses are 300. Theoretically, I should be 250 short every month. But I don't know where it comes from – it just appears."

At thirty-two, Andrei was on the uppermost edge of this generation; he had had time to work and make a family before perestroika – rendering escape from civilization more difficult for him than it was for his unencumbered friends – but he had not had enough time to create a safety net for himself, meaning that he was too young to be in the generation of people who did not dream of escaping their new culture.

Andrei started to learn his trade in second grade. Literally. His elementary school in Kaliningrad – a Russian exclave in Lithuania – had a technical "specialization," so he learned to assemble radios, which he went on to do at a factory, in the Army in Afghanistan, then in the KGB, where he worked while he studied toward a degree in radio engineering. For him the secret police was merely a job and a guarantee of his family's welfare, as it had been for his father and grandfather. It never even occurred to him he might not work there some day. The moment that thought finally came to him – at the dawn of perestroika – he quit his job and moved to Leningrad. He got a job at a factory, which stopped production in 1988, when war broke out in the Azeri region that had supplied raw materials. Andrei and his wife, a photographer, formed one of the newly legal private companies and began earning decent money shooting weddings and other private celebrations. But the fall of the Berlin Wall ended the supply of cheap East German film. Andrei's wife, an ethnic German with a birthright to emigrate, decided she had had enough of the Russian rollercoaster and left. Andrei, a statistically average representative of the provincial intelligentsia, did not wish to leave.

"So 1991 was the beginning of a period when money started coming from nowhere and disappearing into nowhere too. Any attempt to earn money ended in nothing. Furthermore, there was a direct correlation: the more effort I put into earning money, the less the return."

Andrei remarried and gradually grew into the role of manager for his second wife, an artist. For a time, her work sold and they could survive for half a year off one sale. Then the Russian art market collapsed as suddenly and completely as it had appeared. Since then Andrei, his wife and her two daughters had eaten mostly pasta and otherwise economized in every way.

Still, there were no complaints. Moreover, Andrei's statements on his lifestyle bore a striking resemblance to the philosophy espoused by the Western Generation X – corrected, of course, for Russian reality, which often renders Western popular tragedies as a farce. The root, of course, was not in the absence of jobs in general or an art market in particular. The root was in the value system, which Andrei related to me gradually over the course of the day he and I spent together – as he pointed out with evident pleasure, his chosen lifestyle allowed him never to have to rush.

"You see, the situations we have set up for ourselves are based on the ideas imbued in us thanks to the population that can still call itself the intelligentsia. Now we can say that these ideas are not applicable. But we don't want to part with them either." They had none of the intelligentsia's drive and passion. They did not even carry on its guilt. But they had preserved its life habits, its relationships to the everyday, in perfect detail.

"For people who have gone into business, every day is an investment in their future. For me every day has its own value, and I try to take advantage of it. If your head isn't filled up with stuff, then you are open to new experiences, impressions – especially in this city. All you have to do is step outside –

"I think the theory that a person should work toward his future is not guaranteed mistake-free. We've already been burned on this. No one plans to be worse off five years down the road. Everyone tries to up his benchmark, and ending up below the mark is a catastrophe. Learning not to plan for your future is a part of the process of liberating yourself from illusions that were forced on us by our parents, by society. To plan is to create new stereotypes. Having rid ourselves of a set of stereotypes, we should not go about creating new ones."

Those seemed like appropriate last words on this generation. If the *shestidesiatniki* engaged their society in as constructive a way as they could fathom and the intelligentsia of the 1970s defiantly staked out an existence outside the larger society's frameworks, then the Russian Generation X refused to define itself in any relationship to society at all. By rejecting newspapers and other momentary information, they rid themselves not only of any pain they might have felt for losing their rights to participate in society, but also of any feeling of responsibility for what happened around them. "I don't even pay taxes," Yulia told me proudly. "I bear no responsibility whatsoever for what these assholes do."

In theory these people – the well-educated, talented and free-thinking men and women – should have been planning not only their own but their society's future. They should have been setting new standards in politics, science and art. They were at the age when they could make their greatest contribution to the country and its culture. Their predecessors in the 1970s, while refusing to engage with their environment, continued to create – for themselves and their friends. This generation took the disengagement a step further. Andrei and his artist friends came up with a new kitchen-table game: instead of painting pictures, they would describe them. All of us remembered a haunting photograph from our school textbooks: black and white, a grave, a dilapidated house, and an old woman in tears, captioned, A FASCIST FLEW OVER. Andrei described: vivid color, a dilapidated house, a grave, a woman in tears, captioned, A NEW RUSSIAN FLEW OVER. It was a barrel of laughs at the kitchen table, but it left no traces.

CHAPTER ELEVEN

THE BAD GENERATION

On the occasion of fleeing his homeland, journalist Yaroslav Mogutin threw a fabulous party. On March 15, 1995, in the center of Moscow, in a large room that served as the studio of Mogutin's husband, New York expatriate artist Robert Filippini, the French consul-general and a second secretary in the US Embassy rubbed elbows with scandalously famous writer cum far-right activist Eduard Limonov, leading alternative fashion designer Nikolai Polushkin, the country's most successful theater director, Roman Viktiuk, and countless journalists straddling the line between being friends of the host and documenters of the news with a drunken lack of finesse. Two people with a Betacam and a furry mic suspended over the stylish crowd made no bones about seeing the going-away party as a news event as they worked their way through to Mogutin's mother and sister, who looked lost pinned to the lone couch. Above them hung one of Filippini's Russian text pieces, which had just acquired its ironic twist after a couple of years in existence: WHAT IS IT ABOUT THIS PLACE THAT HOLDS YOU HERE?

Around ten, when the *beau monde* concentration reached its peak, Mogutin, a six-foot-tall blue-eyed vision in post-pubescent gay male perfection clad in a motorcycle jacket and an "X" baseball cap, requested a moment of attention to frame his and Filippini's sudden departure. "I am twenty years old," Mogutin declared, quoting his own open letter distributed to the media a few days earlier. "For three of those years I have been working in journalism, and for a year and a half I have faced a real danger of ending up behind bars. . . . I dared to express my opinion – the opinion of a Russian patriot – about the events in Chechnya, and they cannot forgive me for this. I am being forced out of my country."

A theatrical embrace between teary-eyed Mogutin and three-sheets-to-the-wind Limonov followed, and shortly the guests formed a trickle from the apartment to Moscow's more expensive nightclubs, leaving behind thirty-two empty bottles and a half-dozen mellow die-hards. Half-lying on the couch, Polushkin, the conceptual fashion designer, tried to impart to me his vision of the world: most people, he explained, are like "blind kittens in a labyrinth, scared and struggling, while only a few manage not to dissolve in the mob." Oddly, in the next room, Russia's AIDS poster boy, Gennady Roshupkin, was engaged in an intense dialogue on the relationship of the individual to the mob. At this party in this city, where it was more often the Mob – not the mob, and certainly not the individual – that generated party chatter, the host's ability to stand out was the main conversation piece.

In fact, it seemed to be the goal of the host's life. "I realize this is just your latest publicity stunt," a reporter for Moscow's business daily said to Mogutin in parting. Mogutin projected instant outrage: "To think that I would put myself in the position of being forced out of the country just for the sake of another media scandal?" That would be bizarre – true – but not at all out of character. Despite his tender age and a profession that hardly offers a direct route to celebrity, Mogutin had managed to string fifteen-minute segments into a nearly continuous media presence over the couple of years preceding his departure. Mogutin's husband, Filippini, had been right behind him. To their credit, the couple had a highly publicized wedding, covered in scores of Russian and Western publications; a show of Filippini's conceptual art that had a piece in which he claimed to have SUCKED OFF MALEVICH beamed into every household in Russia; dozens of controversial articles by and two lawsuits against Mogutin, the latter of which had now forced the duo to leave Moscow for New York.

Mogutin painstakingly crafted the public persona of a man who takes nothing seriously – except the crafting of his public persona. His doubtless remarkable short biography grew over with myth-making details rendered believable only by repetition. The persona was a self-made man, the miracle child of a seamstress and a drunk from a backwoods village of 3,000 who had lived in Moscow on his own since the age of fifteen (some printed sources said thirteen); Mogutin himself was the son of a children's writer and a former television journalist, now a businesswoman, from a small town a couple of hours outside of Moscow; he had in fact come to Moscow at fifteen but then returned home to finish high school. Of course, then he took Moscow by force, becoming a household name – and the minor adjustments to his biography had probably done less to advance his career than to increase his self-confidence. Infatuated with his own image, he not only drew inspiration from it, he believed it, to the point that he told his stock stories even after he knew I'd interviewed his mother.

But it was a good thing Mogutin loved himself as much as he did. Otherwise, he might have been unable to stand up to the amount of bile that the Moscow journalist community directed his way. By the time Mogutin prepared to leave the country, it was *de rigueur* to trash him on the pages of the major Russian publications, such as the daily *Sevodnia* (Today) and the weeklies *Obshaya gazeta* (The Common Newspaper) and *Stolitsa* (The Capital). It was not the fact that Mogutin was young, pretty and talented that kept the journalistic establishment up at night; it was that he was gloriously unencumbered by principles. He had ridden to prominence on such vehicles as "How I Was a Thief in Paris", a Genet-inspired confessional, and "How I was a Thief in America", a self-referential sequel. He had playfully faced trial on charges of hooliganism – a threat of up to five years in prison – for an article that consisted primarily of profanities. His last achievement on native soil consisted of writing a blatantly racist, chauvinistic piece about the war in Chechnya. Through it all, he exhibited a childlike innocence in refusing to consider the consequences of his words – except, of course, the consequences for his fame. In his utter self-absorption and complete freedom not only from fear but from moral limitations, he was one of the very first representative voices of a new generation of Russians – and this scared the living hell out of that part of his audience that was over twenty-five.

Another person who spoke for this generation, twenty-two-year-old Alina Vitukhnovskaya, was just then complaining to a friend that the media were doing her image a disservice. She was becoming something of a celebrity, but she found her portraits distorted. She suggested someone else should write about her – someone like Mogutin. She could not have known that Mogutin was at this point busy publicizing his exile; she was in jail.

Vitukhnovskaya, child genius, poetic wonder, author of beautiful words of fear, had emerged from the affected Moscow underground with a give-your-morals-a-rest attitude similar to Mogutin's (though the two young people had never met). As a teenager, she saw her poems published in major magazines and newspapers. When she was twenty, Vitukhnovskaya self-published her first book, a black volume titled *Anomalisms*, a heart-rending notebook of obsession with mortality. A year later a Moscow publishing house brought out a book of her poetry, *The Children's Book of the Dead*, a bigger black book populated with mutilated stuffed toys and masterfully twisted quotes from Russian classics. She also started writing articles for *Novoye vriemia* (New Times), a staid weekly magazine edited and read by some of the last of the dissidents. In the fall of 1994 she penned a matter-of-fact exposé of the youth drug culture, a sort of introduction to LSD.

The lack of any judgmental notes in her depictions of psychedelics for the uninitiated was a rare sort of genuine: it stemmed from a true absence. Like Mogutin and others in their generation, Vitukhnovskaya was incapable of trading in moral categories. Her portrayals, like her perceptions, were limited to the realm of the aesthetic, and aesthetic affinity served as her sole guide anywhere, not just in art. Russian literature, with its moral and often moralizing tradition, hardly lent itself to this sort of approach. But like Mogutin, the remarkably talented Vitukhnovskaya had inevitably crossed a line past which society – meaning not only the reading public but the police and the courts – takes one seriously, whether or not one is capable of doing that oneself.

Going out from the center on one of Moscow's main thoroughfares, Leningradskoye shosse, there is a set of four sixteen-story brick apartment towers connected by an intricate chain of archways, porches and barriers, each of which, in the crime-obsessed Moscow of the mid-1990s, promised to be hiding at least one thug. A friend of mine referred to this conglomeration as "The Killers' Quarter." True to her nose for the proper aesthetic setting, Alina Vitukhnovskaya lived in one of these towers – the one with the oddest-shaped porch behind a low wall and no light over the entrance. On October 16, 1994, Alina Vitukhnovskaya was coming home late in the evening when three cars pulled up to the entrance; ten or fifteen men jumped out, grabbed the tiny twenty-one-year-old and pushed her into one of the built-in nooks.

These officers of the FSB – the Federal Security Service, a KGB successor – had come to search the Vitukhnovskys' fifteenth-floor flat because, as it turned out later, Alina was already set up to face drug charges. As Vitukhnovskaya recalled just over a year later, the officers entered the apartment and inquired after "weapons, drugs and poisonous substances."

"I immediately started turning it all into a play, without even knowing what it all meant," Alina told me. "I turned on music and turned off the lights as soon as they walked in. And I thought, 'If this is going to be absurd, then it calls for some aesthetic framing.'" So she mentally reviewed the contents of her tiny room – a stereo system, dozens of pirate-production audiotapes, a fold-out armchair that serves as the bed, one bedside table, one huge garbage-dump mirror and chair to match, and three bookcases that mix classics with computer art – and offered, suddenly remembering: "And do you wish for some ptomaine?" (It was an old story – she had threatened suicide and some friends had promised to make ptomaine from a departed hamster and they had brought it and she had kept it even though she knew it was toothpowder or something equally harmless; still she offered it up to the officers – for show, of course. They entered it into the arrest record, even though it later did turn out to be toothpowder or something equally harmless.)

According to Alina, there were no drugs in the flat. The officers produced them, though – as they produced two scared teenagers who claimed to have bought drugs from Vitukhnovskaya that evening. Later, at the jail, the officers finally produced their demands: they wanted the names of young drug users with "influential" parents.

The FSB had concluded she possessed that sort of information based on her article in *Novoye vriemia*, a piece written largely on hearsay, what Vitukhnovskaya called "disco gossip." To think that for committing this gossip to paper in an obscure magazine a girl from a nice intelligentsia family would spend a year in jail – the absurdity of this could have proved too much for someone with far more experience and ability to adjust. But the twenty-one-year-old fearful depressive girl said she figured out within days what had happened: "It may all have started with that phrase," she said, pointing at eyeliner scribbles on the wallpaper just above her bed: MAKE ME THE HERO OF YOUR COMIC STRIP. "You see, a couple of months before it all happened I was here with a friend and we wrote that. And that may be where it all began."

Like probably any very young very intelligent person – especially one fully aware of the spiritual void left by the collapse of Soviet ideology and its opposites – she was fond of aphorisms in general. She had coined another one: "I am in the media, therefore I am." She had tried to live by it, as had Mogutin – a way of shaping one's identity that proved exceedingly dangerous.

Mogutin appeared on the Moscow publishing scene in the early 1990s as the adorable and perilously youthful lover of a prominent publishing-house owner. He worked for the publisher and lived with him, and the publisher introduced him to the literati and directed his career. "I saw him as someone who could stabilize my life. And he did a lot for me. I quit drinking and started doing journalism and working at the publishing house. I never had a shred of emotion for him, but he loved me." Mogutin smiled innocently. In his value-free world, there was nothing shameful or even remarkable about taking advantage of an older established man.

Mogutin began publishing in *Stolitsa*, a popular weekly magazine. He contributed interviews with celebrities, in large part also older gay men, who seemed to melt in the presence of the cherubic-faced interviewer, giving him the kind of quotes that not only sold magazines but advanced the cause of gay visibility in Russia by leaps and bounds.

Then, in the summer of 1992, Mogutin went to Paris at the invitation of Eduard Limonov, whose books he had helped see to publication. His impressions congealed into an article called "How I Was a Thief in Paris: A True Story With an Unhappy Beginning and End," also published in *Stolitsa*.

"It was reprinted all over the place, including Israel. I got an avalanche of letters, some from repentant thieves and others from outraged readers: 'Lowlife, bastard, who do you think you are – a Russian Jean Genet?'" This clearly beat doing celebrity interviews. Mogutin began to bask in the limelight. He followed the article with more outrageous confessionals – like "Tits in Dough," a heartbreaking tale of helplessly watching nightly rapes and violence while working as a DJ in a village club – shock-value political commentary like "Bitches Big and Small," a rabidly misogynist look at Russia's female politicians, and, of course, "How I Was a Thief in America: A Remake." He claimed to steal everything the West had to offer, from expensive clothes to supermarket sunglasses and compact discs. "But the rush passes." Did he ever steal in Russia? I asked him when he got to New York. "Stealing in Russia doesn't turn me on one bit. There, everyone steals, from the laborer and the collective farmer to the head of state. I always wanted least of all to be like everyone, like the mob, and there, through the very fact of stealing, I would be putting myself on the same level with all the little thieves."

(Sitting down for our first long interview, on Aeroflot's Moscow–New York run, Mogutin asked to know what I had and how I envisioned writing about him "so we can work together." I offered up some notes as a safe sacrifice to his need to control. He reviewed them carefully. Toward the end, his eyes suddenly lit up when he caught the words "Jean Genet complex." "How did you know?" he exclaimed, but caught himself immediately. "I mean, I read him for the first time only recently. Long after I wrote 'How I Was a Thief in Paris.'" His quest for originality led him to the cheapest of tricks: "I was the first journalist to be photographed naked!" he declared with genuine pride.)

But the real break, the accident of fate that would help make Mogutin a household name throughout the country and not just among Moscow media mavens, came in January 1994, when he entered into a mutually

beneficial relationship with another globe-trotting troublemaker. Robert Filippini had landed in Moscow on a lark, after gaining a huge settlement in a lawsuit against his former employer

Theirs was a match made in heaven. A twenty-year-old (though he said he was nineteen) Russian man of letters and an American twenty-one years his senior who made textual art. Neither spoke the other's language. Both loved to hear themselves talk. Each had so much confidence in his own interpretation of events that he never stopped to consider that his partner may view them differently. The language barrier ensured that neither had to. Which just may be the secret of a perfect marriage.

They connected through a mutual friend, an artist who was working on a series of Mogutin portraits. The journalist had just left the publisher, as he had done repeatedly over the years, and was staying in a flat that belonged to Viktiuk, the theater director. "That was a trashy place, so I moved in with Robert and started living like a human being" is how Mogutin recalled the beginning of their romance. "We courted each other. It was beautiful. Then, within a few weeks, we were living together. We were so happy we wanted to pinch ourselves." That's Filippini's version.

Both agreed that the idea of the wedding appeared on its rightful birthday: Valentine's Day, 1994. "I remember it perfectly. I was standing on a chair hanging a curtain in the kitchen. And I said, 'Mogutin, we oughta get married.' And he looked at me and said, 'Sure.' You know how it is when you are so happy you want to pinch yourself?"

"We were sitting in the kitchen drinking tea. Robert was smoking those cigarettes of his [he rolled them]. Then all of a sudden he said, 'We oughta get married.' I said, 'How?' – and because it seemed like such an act of hooliganism, such provocation, I didn't have a good idea of how it could be done, but nonetheless I said, 'All right, let's, but we have to announce it to the press so that no one beats us to it.'" From this point on, Mogutin had trouble with the story. It's not that he didn't remember; it's that he couldn't concentrate on the love story when the events had such a profound impact on his public image, which, to him, was the most interesting subject of all. "For the next two months international press agencies kept calling, asking if the wedding was still on, if we hadn't changed our minds."

"We'll talk about the press reaction in a minute, Slava," I said, using the standard diminutive of his name, which happens to mean "fame." (While we are on the subject: his last name – his real last name – means "mighty.") I tried to get him to talk about the private aspect of the marriage. We backtracked to the proposal. "OK, so at first I didn't quite know what he meant, but then I realized what a great media opportunity it was. Over the next couple of months, all these people kept calling to suggest a group action. But I took offense at that. I said, 'If you are so smart, why didn't you think of it first?'"

So it was a competition? "What Robert offered me was a human thing, because he experienced – and continues to experience – certain feelings for me, and I thought about it and I thought, 'There is nothing wrong with that, I have nothing against it. I would like to enter into a spousal relationship with this person.'" It was unclear whether he was speaking about calculating potential publicity points or overcoming the feelings of shame owning his gay relationship publicly might entail. Probably, a little of both. "I love him," he added.

The press release, nay wedding announcement, capitalized on the couple's joint publicity assets, reminding the viewing audience that Filippini had SUCKED OFF MALEVICH and giving Mogutin's adjusted birth date and other biographical titbits. The wedding was set for April 12, Mogutin's twenty-first (he said twentieth) birthday, which also happens to be Cosmonaut's Day, allowing the birthday boy to nickname himself Space Child and to claim the holiday as "the day of remembering a single man in the strange Cosmos."

Both remembered being nervous on their wedding day. "We were so fucking nervous," confessed Filippini. "We didn't know what was going to happen. We didn't know whether the *militsia* [police] were going to show up, or whether they were going to queue us up in the eternal Russian queue."

"We were really nervous," Mogutin concurred. "We were sitting in the kitchen and I said, 'If we get there and there are only two or three Russian journalists, who have nothing better to do, I don't know what

I'll do.' The thing we feared most was not that we would be denied registration but that we would not draw the media."

He should have had no fear. There were between fifty and seventy (he said a hundred) reporters and photographers at the Civic Registry Office Number 4, where mixed marriages are officiated. The story ran in nearly every Russian newspaper and on every television station, moved on all three major international wires, and netted the couple detailed profiles in such US biggies as the *Los Angeles Times*, the *Philadelphia Inquirer* and the *San Francisco Chronicle*. It was a good story: it highlighted the absurdities built into bureaucracies in the way only outrageous human acts can. First, the grooms-to-be marched to the US Embassy in Moscow to ask for the affidavit required of American citizens desiring to marry Russians. Though Filippini conscientiously drew the clerk's attention to "the gender of the persons involved," the embassy official dispensed the affidavit without blinking an eye. With that in hand the grooms, both clad in black leather jackets, presented themselves to several score journalists and a Civic Registry Office director named Carmen, who told them she had nothing against their union but had found a clause in a 1967 rule book that banned same-sex marriages. She suggested they take their cause to Parliament. Topped with a two-cake – birthday and wedding – party in Filippini's studio, this was quality troublemaking for the media, incontrovertible proof that they were.

But trouble is as trouble does, and soon the two men found themselves in more of it than either of them could have predicted – one because he had grown up in the Land of the Free, and the other because he had never taken either himself or his surroundings seriously. There had been hooliganism charges pending against Mogutin for several months – for a profanity-filled interview with a famous gay dancer, Boris Moiseyev – but Mogutin, having secured the *pro bono* services of the country's most famous defense attorney (who was doing a personal favor for Viktiuk, the theater director), was none too concerned about a minor charge he seemed to view as yet another press opportunity. As it happened, the hearing was scheduled for April 14, just two days after the wedding.

The wake-up call sounded like a doorbell on the evening after the wedding night. The newlyweds were in the kitchen, having supper with two friends. The local cop burst in with two men in civvies. They demanded to see everyone's documents. One of the guests had no passport on him and was taken to the station. At two in the morning the cop returned with a drunk man dressed in a cinematic black leather trench coat, whom the couple came to know and detest and refer to as Scarface, owing to the large scar across half of his face. The cop left while Scarface stayed for a few hours, drinking the couple's vodka and otherwise making himself at home. Finally, he demanded $150 to settle the matter and left.

The next day was Mogutin's day in court. Despite his famous lawyer's best efforts – he argued that his client had been singled out for his sexuality – the case not only was not dropped but was transformed into a more serious charge, "aggravated hooliganism marked by particular cynicism and great impertinence," a perfectly amusing and apparently appropriate charge if only it did not carry a punishment of up to five years in prison. The case was referred to the prosecutor's office for further investigation, to hang over Mogutin's head for the next six months.

At home Mogutin and Filippini were greeted by the local cop, another one in civvies, to be followed at one in the morning by Scarface, this time introducing another regular character, the Pretty Brute. They stayed for hours; the vodka came out again. Also on the kitchen table was a filthy handkerchief stuffed with hash, which Scarface had pulled out of his pocket. In case the message wasn't clear, he reinforced it with a declaration that is one of the few things both Mogutin and Filippini remember identically word-for-blood-chilling-word: "You don't understand. We can do anything we want to you. We can force you out of the country. We can have you committed to a psychiatric hospital."

"You know what happens?" Filippini asked me, shifting into the second-person of necessary alienation. "You lose all your dignity. You become like an animal. You are afraid in your own home."

There were four or five visits over the course of a few days. Finally, the couple appealed to higher police authorities and apparently succeeded in stopping the harassment.

They returned to what should have been their honeymoon cocoon empty and spent. Friends told me the events plunged Mogutin into a dark depression. He told colleagues that professionally he felt used up, having achieved everything he'd set out to – fame, access to publications, the ability to publish in a variety of genres – by the age of twenty. Personally, he also felt pushed into a corner: Both he and Filippini said they could not go outside without being recognized.

As Mogutin searched for a project to latch on to, a friend approached him with the offer to teach in a new program for students of the journalism department at Moscow State University. Then the scholarly board of the university suddenly canceled the program. Credible leaks had it that the real cause was Mogutin's presence among the instructors.

Though Mogutin maintained that the self-imposed isolation of Genet's final years was a fate that appealed to him, he did not seem to be enjoying the setbacks. In any case, his isolation from the fiercely fraternal Moscow journalism community wasn't self-imposed; it was the ugly flip side of his notoriety. Everyone knew of him, and few people thought well of him and his work. At *Novoye vriemia,* where I then worked, he was generally referred to as the Bastard.

Perhaps, in his self-love, Mogutin was oblivious to this. Or maybe he wasn't, and that is why his latest and final prank so resembled a bucket of bile poured out at the first available opportunity, which happened to be the war in Chechnya. In early January, *Novy vzgliad* (New View), an off-color weekly, published an article by Mogutin entitled "The Chechen Knot: 13 Theses." Thirteen targets of unbridled vitriol: the Chechen people, the military, the government, the human rights commissioner, the intelligentsia, and everyone else.

There did not appear to have been anyone in Moscow, except Filippini (who read it in translation long after publication), who liked the article. Mogutin's own mother said "it was a bit harsh." His lawyer looked consternated and, choosing words with extreme, time-consuming care, said, "I am far from thrilled by that article. I told him I think it has taste flaws. I do not share the views expressed." Even the editor of *Novy vzgliad* found "three of the theses repulsive, unacceptable . . ."

Those were his friends. His enemies were far more emphatic, displaying the full array of tools still available for destroying someone for what he said. The Presidential Court Chamber on Information Disputes held two full-scale hearings (the first one fell on Valentine's Day) – with representatives of all allegedly liberal newspapers taking part – to consider the article. It concluded that Mogutin had violated the Constitution and should be tried for inflaming national enmity. The hearing was broadcast on public television, going out to 98 percent of Russia's households, just as I SUCKED OFF MALEVICH had a couple of years earlier. The major newspapers made hay of it; writing in the weekly *Vek*, the secretary of the Journalists' Union stopped just short of calling for the death penalty for Mogutin, whom – he made this clear – this colleague deplored as much for his fey appearance as for his views.

As Mogutin's future US lawyer would say a month later, commenting on the merits of his asylum claim in exquisite legalese, "It seemed like they were really out to squash the guy."

The Presidential Court Chamber is what the Soviet system of censorship had devolved into: it was not a part of the judicial system – therefore it was not bound by any due-process requirements – but it was free to take on any case, hear it with or without the defendant present (or even informed), and then make recommendations, which were often heeded by the judicial system (this being a presidential body, after all). In this case the Chamber recommended that criminal charges be filed against Mogutin. Which, as his lawyer explained to him, could spell seven years in prison.

"He called me at the studio when he came back. He was lying on the bed staring at the ceiling. 'Robbie,' he said, 'It's a dangerous situation for me.' And this weight in your chest – "

The idea of leaving the country crystallized in a flash, and within a month of this conversation the couple landed in New York. Mogutin asked for political asylum.

Vitukhnovskaya was not granted even the dubious luxury of staring at the ceiling desperately plotting an escape. The dozen men who seized her on October 16 delivered her to her morbid comic-strip existence later that night. She landed in Moscow's infamous Butyrki prison, where since the time of Catherine the Great thousands of poets, dissidents and common criminals had been kept in subhuman conditions, beaten, tortured and driven to sickness and death.

After about six months of interrogations, threats and bizarrely complacent lawyers, Moscow's writing community suddenly noticed her case. The Russian PEN Center took on her defense. Articles began appearing in the major newspapers and magazines, extolling Alina's poetic talent and the injustices to which she was being subjected. Her gift was compared to that of Anna Akhmatova and Marina Tsvetaeva, two great women poets of the twentieth century. Her fate was linked to the eternal cross of the poet in Russia: always in opposition, in disfavor, in peril.

Later, after Vitukhnovskaya was released, she appeared at the presentation of a new newspaper devoted entirely to poetry. The roster was all "name" poets with some dissident credentials; the youngest was twenty years her senior. Vitukhnovskaya was included – had to be included – as the poetic martyr celebrity of the new generation. The patriarch of dissident poets, the grayingly sixties Andrei Voznesenski, made a casual remark about the 1970s: "It was an era after Stalinist camps but before Vitukhnovskaya camps." The audience chuckled respectfully: what neat continuity.

Such facile continuity. Vitukhnovskaya the prisoner could not have been further from the numerous poet and intellectual prisoners who had preceded her. True, they too had been jailed on false premises, often linked to something unsavory like drug dealing or sex crimes. They too had drawn attention to themselves with their words, which became thorns in the system's side. But there the similarities end. The prisoners of old survived on the certainty of their righteousness, on their own vision of themselves as heroes.

A couple of months before Vitukhnovskaya was arrested, she and a close friend spent all night talking about the essence of heroism. "We concluded that heroism is the absolute refusal to admit one's own negligibility. Whereas real heroism is in admitting it. And somebody like Pierrot is a thousand times the hero that someone like Gagarin is." Thus was born the phrase MAKE ME THE HERO OF YOUR COMIC STRIP.

Coming this close to the realization of her own insignificance had always terrified her. Her poetry is a string of expressions of regret at having to be human:

A boring creature. Neither fish nor meat.

Nor a bug (as someone had suggested)
that had power for losing power
is crawling for he has nothing else to do
(just long as no one eats it).
Or let them eat
the untasty bug.
No big loss, yourself.

Or:

4.
Flaking
off some part of the body.
Kremlin is a balm to the capital's residents.
Perhaps I do not reside?

5.
If, for instance, I do become fresh
clean damp ours yours
future young-green
(a sort of meta-super-manly),
that still leaves open the possibility of an involuntary
hiccup or slip.

My Alina Vitukhnovskaya notes begin with a quote: "Of all social definitions – man, woman, child – I would take child." A bit later she clarified, saying that at the age of six she realized that the world into which she had been born was real. "And since then I cannot shake off the sensation of horror. I simply cannot be natural; I can only simulate various expressions of humanity." Still later she confessed that what she found hardest was "having to be human – first, and second, having to be mortal. I would agree to be some mythical creature, a creature without sex, age and not subject to aging. It's a childish dream, of course, but what's the point of hiding it if I have it?"

Shoved into the macabre unreality of Russia's oldest jail and having concluded that she had entered a comic strip of her own design, Vitukhnovskaya got to work creating a mythical creature – not devoid of any attributes of humanity, but as far removed from her own sense of self as she could conjure. She described it as one part some German extremist group (she had seen it on videotape), one part French prostitute, and one part the little girl from the Addams Family movies. Even after her release from jail, the look remained her signature; she would arrive at the courthouse wearing a miniskirt with black stockings and extremely high heels, a leopard-print fake-fur car coat, her black frizzy hair loose over her shoulders and down to her waist, and makeup for the spectators in the back row. She smiled incessantly and inappropriately, though she had always known herself to be a depressive given to crying jags.

"See, I had decided that it was all an action and I, as the author of this action, can only act accordingly," she explained, using the word *action* in its Moscow-artsy sense of "street theater." "And of course their behavior was unpredictable, but my design provided for that." So when she was suddenly offered the opportunity to be examined by a court psychiatrist, her design called for her to use her extensive experience of dealing with all manner of shrinks (she'd been the impressionable only child of nervous parents) to impersonate a perfectly healthy person. This could only infuriate the investigators further. As did her sudden declaration one day that she would finally give them the information they sought on the location of a drug laboratory in Moscow.

"In 1943, a certain Swiss chemist working in his laboratory invented LSD," she dictated to three exasperated FSB agents.

For months they called her in for interrogations, saying that she could avoid eight or more years in prison simply by disclosing the location of the lab and the names of drug-using children of influential parents. She did not know where the lab was: she had only heard rumors of its existence, which she cited in her infamous article. But she knew the names they wanted. Why didn't she tell? I asked. They were not even her friends – just people she had seen at discotheques.

"That would have simply been low," she responded, briefly looking hurt by my suggestion. Then she caught herself: "I can't claim that I was guided by moral principles of some sort – I just would have been disgusted. Perhaps it's because the way I acted was the only way I find aesthetically acceptable. I mean, I could start some crazy horrible war, but I could not do something so petty."

The poets and writers and organizers who embraced Alina Vitukhnov-skaya after her arrest could not conceive of this utter lack of moral principles that she stubbornly espoused. Instead of decrying the unfair arrest of a scared little girl, old dissidents and underground artists like the writer Lev Timofeyev and the poet Konstantin Kedrov declared her a political prisoner. Perhaps this was not a lack of compassion as much as it was their own fear. They were as scared of Vitukhnovskaya's moral void framed in talented words as they had been of the same thing with Mogutin. Mogutin had infuriated them, probably in large part because he was male and brash and had escaped truly harsh punishment. Vitukhnovskaya – female, more morbid than rude, and truly long-suffering – left them no choice but to fit her in a moral framework. And they certainly never stopped to think that officialdom could not digest the two harbingers of future minds and hearts for the same reason: officialdom abhors a vacuum because officialdom abhors everything it does not understand; even when it finally became tolerant of all views expressed, it could not tolerate the unplaceable lack of views.

And it certainly could not understand why, if Mogutin and Vitu-khnovskaya did not have the sustenance of deeply felt moral beliefs, they did not simply bend to the system. Why Vitukhnovksaya did not tell them the names. The reason was what Alina called "metaphysical greed."

Isaiah Berlin's description of the Russian intelligentsia as bound by a "collective sense of guilt" may have been the most apt definition of the intelligentsia as a group – but as people they were better defined by their stubborn and irrational belief in individual agency. Thus they could sing, as the playwright and poet Aleksandr Galich did, that his typewriter made four copies "and that's enough." Thus they could claim, as the scholar and politician Galina Starovoitova did, to be protected by a "shield of justice."

Their descendants, the children with no faith, had nothing to shield them. Only constant resonance could keep their fear at bay. Only seeing their own reflections, only perfecting them, only the mass media could prove to them that they existed. They had to be heroes – but only of comic strips.

7.
I am truly scared,
and so I am not a hero of your time
(fear exceeds individuality).

Their dismissive aesthetic placed their selves in parenthesis. One could finally conclude that the last of the intelligentsia had rendered itself dead.

Except what form of protest and call to difference was available in a society as charged with politics as Russia in the 1990s, other than a retreat to the purely aesthetic? And what was this insistent obliteration of self if not self-sacrifice?

Vintage intelligentsia. A new vintage.

SELECTED BIBLIOGRAPHY

Ludmila Alekseyeva, *Istoriya inakomysliya v SSSR* (A History of Dissidence in the USSR), Vilnius-Moscow: Vest', 1992.

Ludmila Alekseyeva and Paul Goldberg, *The Thaw Generation*, Boston, London and Toronto: Little, Brown, 1990.

Alexander Babyonyshev (ed.), *On Sakharov*, New York: Alfred A. Knopf, 1982.

Isaiah Berlin, *Russian Thinkers*, Harmondsworth, Middlesex: Penguin Books, 1978.

Yelena Bonner, *Dochki-materi* (Mothers and Daughters), New York: Chekhov, 1990.

Yelena Bonner, *Postscriptum* (English title: *Alone Together*), New York: Chekhov, 1990.

Douglas Coupland, *Generation X: Tales for an Accelerated Culture*, New York: St Martin's Press, 1991.

Boris Dubin and Lev Gudkov, *Intelligentsia. Zametki o literaturno-politicheskikh illuziyakh* (The Intelligentsia: Notes on Literary-Political Illusions), Moscow: Epitsentr and Kharkov: Folio, 1995.

Savely Dudakov, *Istoriya odnogo mifa* (The History of a Myth), Moscow: Nauka, 1993.

Sergei Gandlevsky, "Trepanatsiya cherepa" (Skull Trephination), *Znamia*, Issue 1, 1995.

Mikhail Gorbachev, *Zhizn i reformy* (My Life and Reforms) Moscow: Novosti, 1995.

Mikhail Gorbachev, *Perestroika i novoye myshleniye* (Perestroika and New Thinking), Moscow: Izdatelstvo politicheskoy literatury, 1987.

Leonid Gozman and Alexander Etkind, *The Psychology of Post-Totalitarianism in Russia*, London: Centre for Research into Communist Economies, 1992.

Mikhail Heller, *Sedmoy sekretar. Blesk i nisheta Mikhailia Gorbacheva* (The Seventh Secretary: The Gloss and Poverty of Mikhail Gorbachev), Moscow: MIK, 1995.

Mikhail Heller and Alexander Nekrich, *Utopia u vlasti. Istoriya sovetskogo gosudarstva s 1917 goda do nashikh dney* (Utopia in Power: A History of the Soviet State from 1917 to the Present), London: Overseas Publications Interchange, 1982.

Andrei Karaulov, *Plokhoi malchik* (The Bad Boy), Moscow: Sovershenno sekretno, 1996.

Vladimir Lakshin, *Berega kultury* (The Banks of Culture), Moscow: Miros, 1994.

Dmitry Likhachev, *Vospominaniya* (Memoirs), St Petersburg: Logos, 1995.

Anatoly Marchenko, *Zhivi kak vse* (To Live Like Everyone), Moscow: Vest-VIMO, 1993.

Michael Meerson-Aksenov and Boris Shragin (eds), *The Political, Social and Religious Thought of Russian "Samizdat"*, Belmont, MA: Nordland Publishing Co., 1977.

Yury Nagibin, *T'ma v kontse tunelia* (Darkness at the End of the Tunnel), Moscow: Sovetsky pisatel, 1994.

Yury Nagibin, *Dnevnik* (Journal), Moscow: Knizhny sad, 1995.

Yuri Orlov, *Opasniye mysli. Memuary iz russkoy zhizni* (Dangerous Ideas: A Memoir of Life in Russia), Moscow: Argumenty i fakty, 1992.

Raisa Orlova, *Vospominaniya o neproshedshem vremeni* (A Memoir of a Time Not Past), Moscow: Slovo, 1993.

Oleg Poptsov *Khroniki vremion tsaria Borisa* (The Chronicles of the Time of Czar Boris), Moscow: Edition Q, 1996.

Marc Raeff (ed.), *Russian Intellectual History: An Anthology*, New York: Harcourt, Brace & World, 1966.

Andrei Sakharov, *Vospominaniya* (Memoirs), New York: Chekhov Publishing, 1990.

Andrei Sakharov, *Gorky, Moskva, daleye vezde* (Gorky, Moscow, and Everywhere From There), New York: Chekhov Publishing, 1991.

Andrei Sakharov, *Mir, progress, prava cheloveka* (Peace, Progress and Human Rights), Leningrad: Sovetsky pisatel, 1990.

Sergei Sekirinsky and Tatyana Filippova, *Rodoslovnaya rossiyskoy svobody* (The Family Tree of Russian Liberty), Moscow: Vysshaya shkola, 1993.

Igor Shafarevich, "Rusophobia, Sotsialism v mirovoy istorii" (Socialism in World History), in *Collected Works*, Moscow: Fenix, 1994.

Alexander Solzhenitsyn *Bodalsia telionok s dubom* (As the Calf Rammed the Oak Tree), in *Collected Works*, Vermont and Paris: YMCA Press, 1982.

Alexander Solzhenitsyn, *"Russky vopros" k kontsu XX veka* ("The Russian Question" at the End of the Twentieth Century), Moscow: Golos, 1995.

Alexander Solzhenitsyn, *Kak nam obustroit' Rossiyu* (How We Can Revitalize Russia), Leningrad: Sovetsky pisatel, Leningradskoye otdeleniye, 1990.

Vekhi (Milestones) and *Intelligentsia v Rossii* (The Intelligentsia in Russia), Moscow, Molodaya gvardiya, 1991.

Books of poetry

Aleksandr Galich, *Ya vybirayu svobodu*, Moscow: Glagol, Issue 3, 1991.

Sergei Gandlevsky, *Prazdnik*, St Petersburg: Pushkinsky fond, 1995.

Olesya Nikolayeva, *Zdes'*, Moscow: Sovetsky pisatel, 1990.

Yevgeny Saburov, *Porokhovoy zagovor*, Moscow: Zolotoy vek, 1995.

Alina Vitukhnovskaya, *Anomalisms*, Moscow: Mysh, 1993.

INDEX